OTHER MACK STANLEY TITLES
BACK IN PRINT

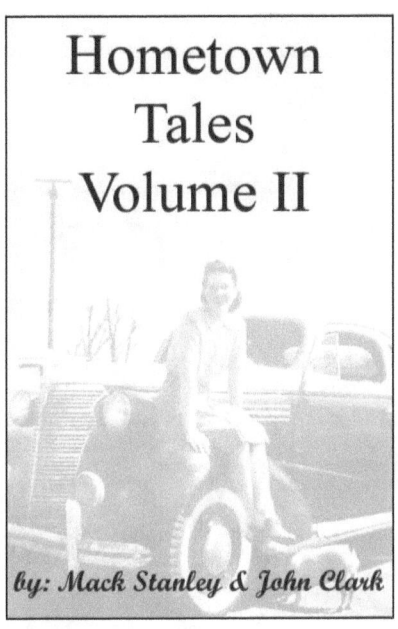

Hometown
Tales
Volume II

by: Mack Stanley & John Clark

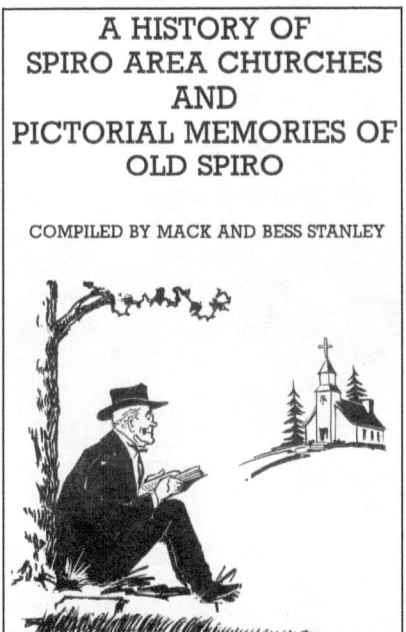

A HISTORY OF
SPIRO AREA CHURCHES
AND
PICTORIAL MEMORIES OF
OLD SPIRO

COMPILED BY MACK AND BESS STANLEY

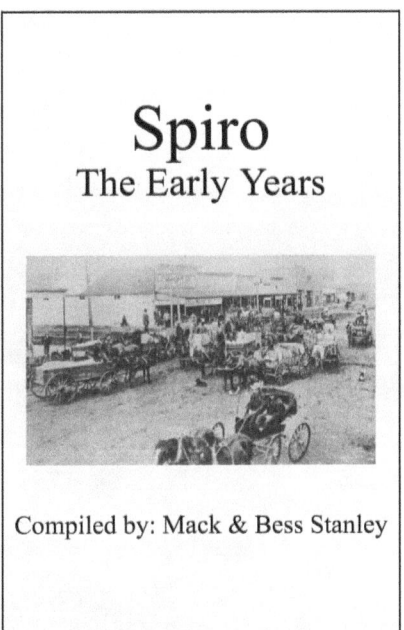

Spiro
The Early Years

Compiled by: Mack & Bess Stanley

www.DissenterPublishing.com

Hometown Tales, Volume I

***

by: Mack Stanley & John Clark

Dissenter Publishing
PROGRESS IN LITERATURE

Hometown Tales Volume I

Materials in the book are licensed for publishing under agreement between Graphic Publishing Inc., and Dissenter Publishing.

Many thanks to the kind folks of Spiro who provided the photos that went into this project. Special thanks to Miss Peggy Crane of the Spiro Historical Society; Jake Smith; The Spiro Graphic; Many friends of Mack Stanley who assisted over the years.

Edited by Kristopher Clark

Published by:

Dissenter Publishing

STE 376 #150

2436 S. I-35E

Denton, TX 76205

www.DissenterPublishing.com

Dissenter Publishing is a DBA of KJ Clark Ventures Corp

ISBN-13: 978-0-9845613-0-8

ISBN-10: 0-9845613-0-7

This is not intended as exact factual history. It is what predominately remains in the attic of my memory. There are usually a few cobwebs in an old attic. Our aim has been to send a small smile or chuckle to as many as we can reach with our lifetime accumulation of "Hometown Tales."

We heard most of these little stories in our old home towns of Spiro, Oklahoma and Fort Smith, Arkansas.

"Hope you find a chuckle here."

Sincerely

Mack Stanley

Bess Stanley

"It is the Lord's blessing that most of us who lived through the Great Depression didn't have sense enough to worry about it."

- Mack Stanley, Spiro, Oklahoma

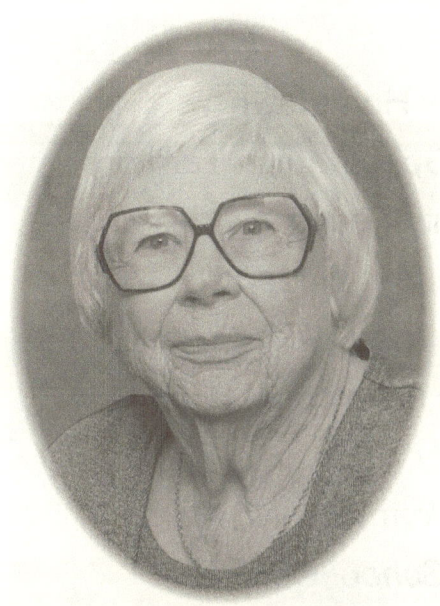

Miss Peggy Crane

Spiro and the surrounding communities lost a great friend in the passing of Peggy Crane in April of 2009.

Known to most everyone as Miss Peggy, she was the 'go-to' person that could be counted on for almost any public event and activity going on in Spiro. Miss Peggy kept the Spiro Museum running and open when there were no funds or volunteers to help. She was very active in the Chamber of Commerce and Spiro VFW Ladies Auxiliary.

Ask yourself: 'What would we have done without her community service? — Remember all the wonderful deeds she gave to Spiro for many years.

On behalf of The Spiro Museum & Historical Society Miss Peggy provided many of the photos published in this book. –John Clark

The Tales

About The Hometown

The town of Spiro came into being in 1898, back when Oklahoma was still known as Indian Territory. Mr. Edgar Moore and two of his kinsmen who owned the land where the town is now located had it surveyed and marked into streets, alleys, and lots.

The first store was built on the lot where we later ran Stanley's Café for many years, at the intersection of Main and Broadway. Cheatham's General Merchandise and Cotton Buyers, which eventually sold out to the Dunklin Bros Corporation. Soon after in September 1898 Redwine Brothers went into business. Mr. RL Redwine had a dry goods store in Hackett, Arkansas and Mr. John Redwine had been a farmer and livestock dealer over there. Their initial store was a short ways north from where, six years later, in 1904 they built the native rock building which today houses the firm of Redwine's Incorporated.

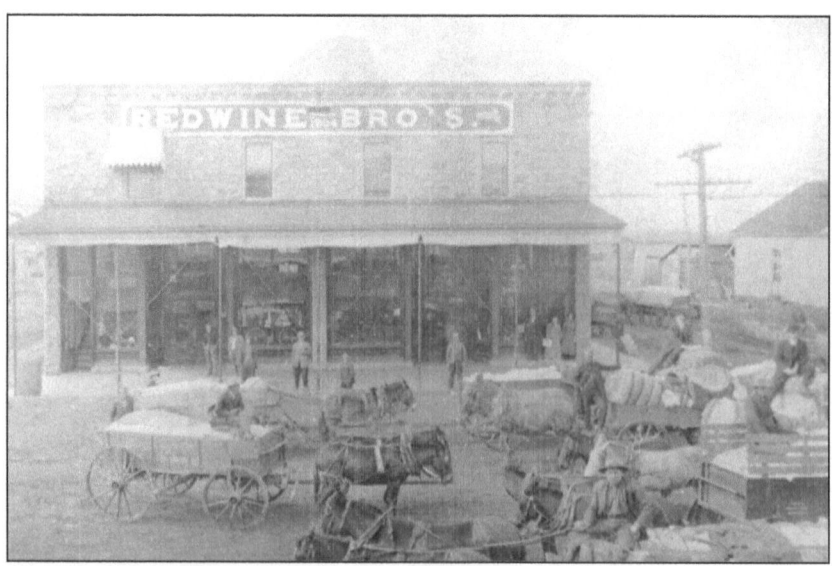

Redwine Bros on Main Street Spiro

The Spiro power house for the light and Water Department was constructed around 1911, which was the tine Burgevin's Branch was dammed to create our Old City Lake.

This coal-burning boiler and the generating turbine served well and long to furnish electricity to Spiro and pump our water. The economy of this energy plant is what kept Spiro running without any city tax, one of only two towns in the country able to operate that ways at that time.

It is ironic that soon after the town replaced the old turbine with a new one, which was very expensive, they switched over to purchasing electricity from a major power company, and had to sell this fine new engine later at a price of only $8,000. Wouldn't it be nice to have some of that cheap energy now?

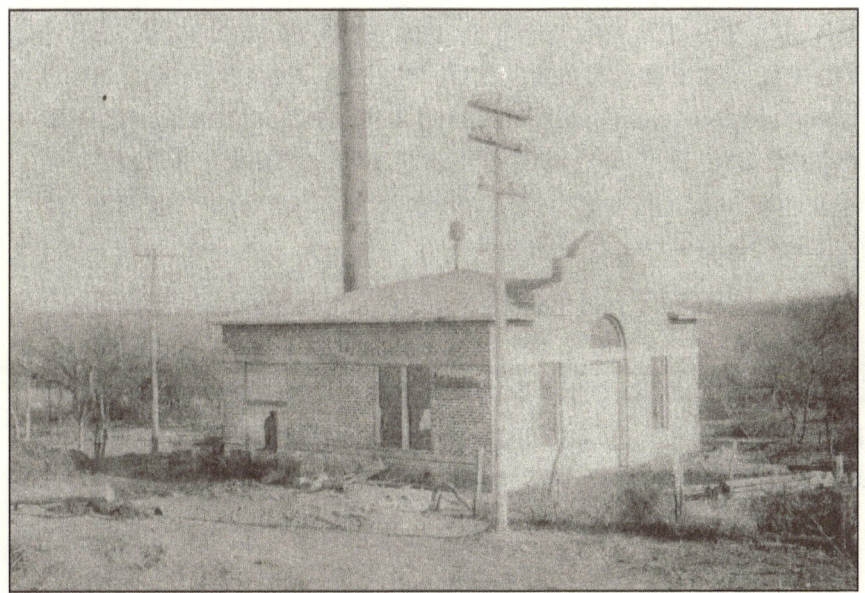

This building still stands today.

The wide Main Street was built for a unique purpose. There were no automobiles in Indian Territory when the town was plotted. Horses and buggies and wagons hauling crops to market were the means of transportation. Women rode sidesaddle.

The wide Main Street was for wagons to turn around in the middle of the street and travel north or south. The cotton gins were owned by Dunklin Brothers and Redwine Brothers.

Today, automobiles park parallel and side-by-side in the middle of Main Street. Traffic flows freely on both sides traveling north and south.

Yes, Spiro was a bustling place in those first few years, which brought it from a bare prairie where hay had been baled, to a full fledged frontier town of some reputation.

For many years it was a typical small western farm town with hitching posts and rails and watering troughs for the horses and mules along the plank sidewalked Main Street and the large hitching lots behind the two largest mercantile stores. There were even some open water wells in the middle of that wide thoroughfare.

About 1920 Redwine Brothers had two cotton gins and Dunklin Brothers had two, but each of these firms had one double gin. There was another gin brought in by an outsider, so that was actually equal to seven cotton gins in this small town.

Oldtimers (those old guys in their 80's) recall that during the rush at the peak of the cotton picking season, the cotton wagons were backed three blocks up Main Street past Redwine's. The street would become blocked by literally hundreds of wagons and teams at times. Spiro was always a good cotton market, many growers brought their fleecy white stuff from as far away as twenty miles.

All the land around this area that would produce was planted mostly to cotton, it seemed. Woods and canebrakes were cleared by backbreaking work and put in cotton. Cotton was King, but year after year of this planting practice eventually robbed the soil of its cotton—growing nutrients and each year it produced less and less bales per acre.

This temporarily damaged the good land, and the king fell from his local throne and snuck off to other lands.

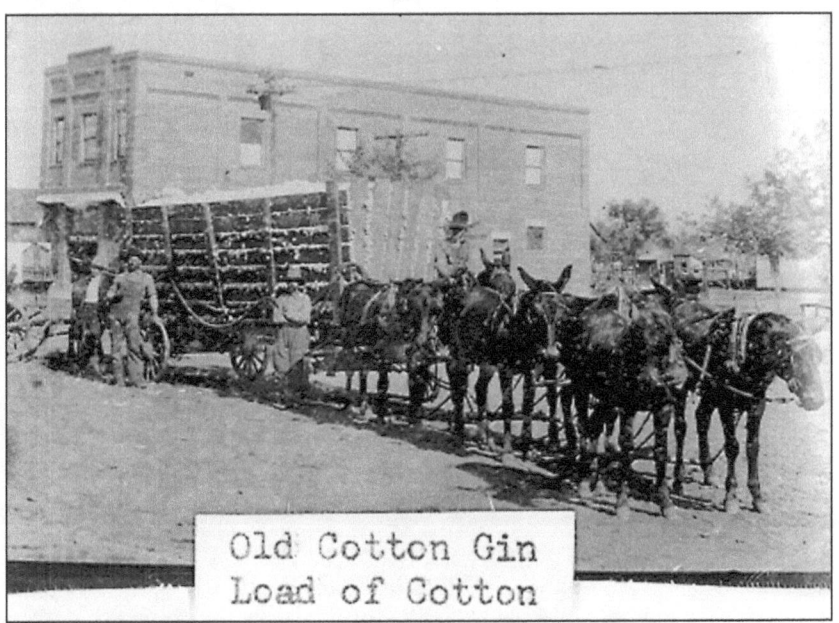

Old Cotton Gin
Load of Cotton

The building in the back still stands today.

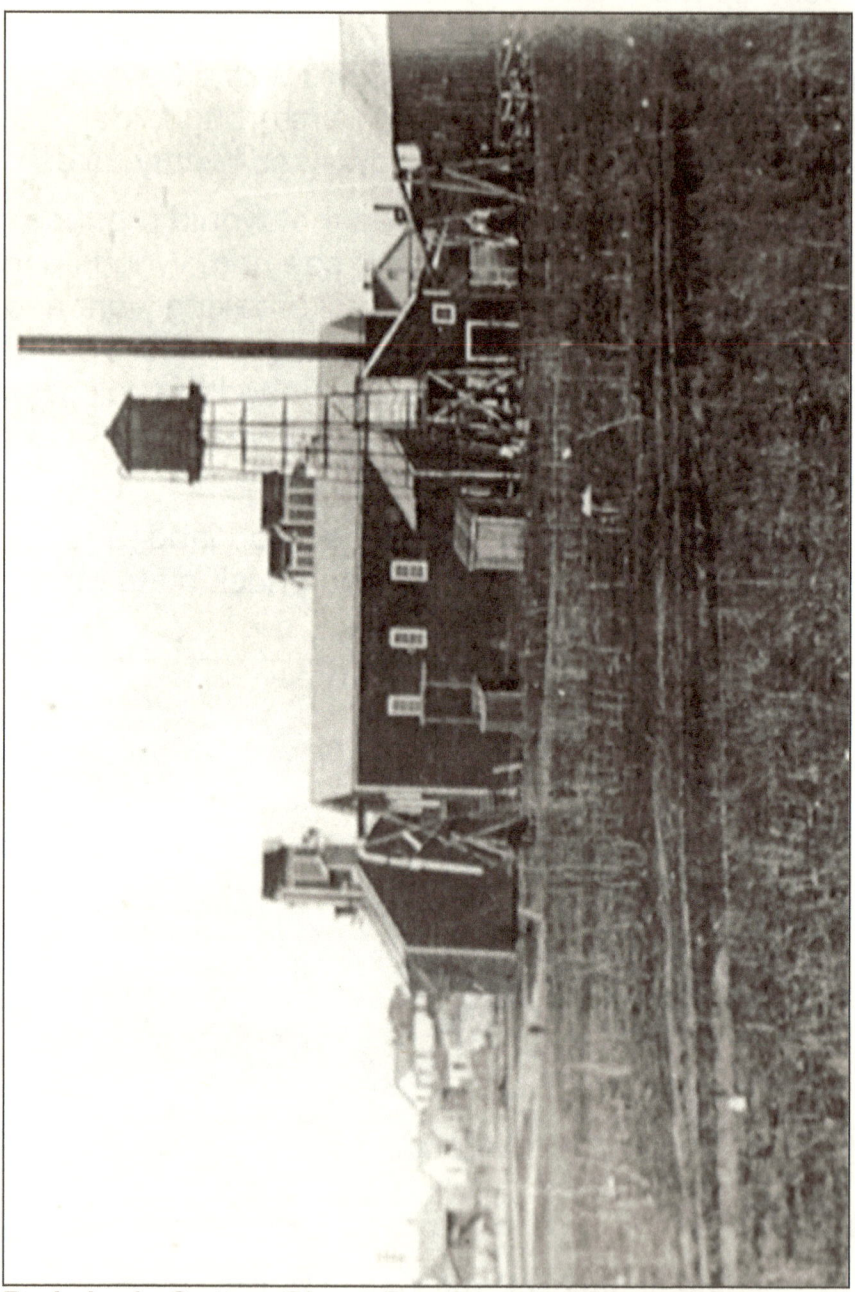

Redwine's Cotton Gin at South end of Main Street

The cotton gins were a quartet, but when things were humming (whining) they made the noise of a full orchestra.

Gone now is the whining song of those old cotton gins. Sometimes their Autumnal song was only an untuneful four month melody that began around the first of September and lasted well through the year-end holidays.

Towns like ours reached their height of activity and population in the early 1920's. Back then, about twenty percent of the population was in towns of smaller than ten thousand people. By the eighth decade of the same century that figure has faltered to almost half that percentage, and is still diminishing.

Gradually, the teams and wagons and buggies of our childhood gave way to faster and noisier automobiles on our roads, and tractors replaced mules in the fields of our farms. This change caused the passing of the blacksmith shop, livery stables, wagon yards, and one prominent part of farm commerce, horse and mule trading. Horse and mule business was big, many family assets were built on this part of business.

The center of women's activity, outside the home was church work, quilting bees. Very little of their time was spent in trivial pursuits. Most grocery shopping was done by phone and orders were delivered to their kitchens. This was where women reigned supreme.

Men, after losing many loafing places due to the advent of the Automobile Age, shifted their loafing places to drug stores, barbershops, pool halls and backbends of small grocery stores. Before radio, then later television, the avenge barbershops were favorite places for men to kill time. The loafers usually outnumbered the customers. Barber- shops were beehives of news and gossip. Barbers were usually the best comedian in town.

Although the inhabitants of every little town were not 'like one big happy family' they were at least totally aware of everyone else in town. You knew the father, the mother of every house in town, their first names and the names of all the kids, dogs, cats and even the milk cow.

In towns like ours, you could live out your life without many exciting things ever happening to you, but it was a pleasant routine and a good way of life. First, we were kids playing out our roles into teenage, then through school and into young adulthood, into and through our first jobs. Then romances into marriages, most times with locals of our own, and on through a long hard-working period into middle age. Finally into senior citizens with reduced activity, and then the inevitable. I suppose that is not so different from average the world over at that time. It was all we knew, so what could we do about it? We simply accepted it as graciously as we could and loved it until the last day.

More history of the hometown can be found in my book "Spiro: The Early Years." – *Mack Stanley*

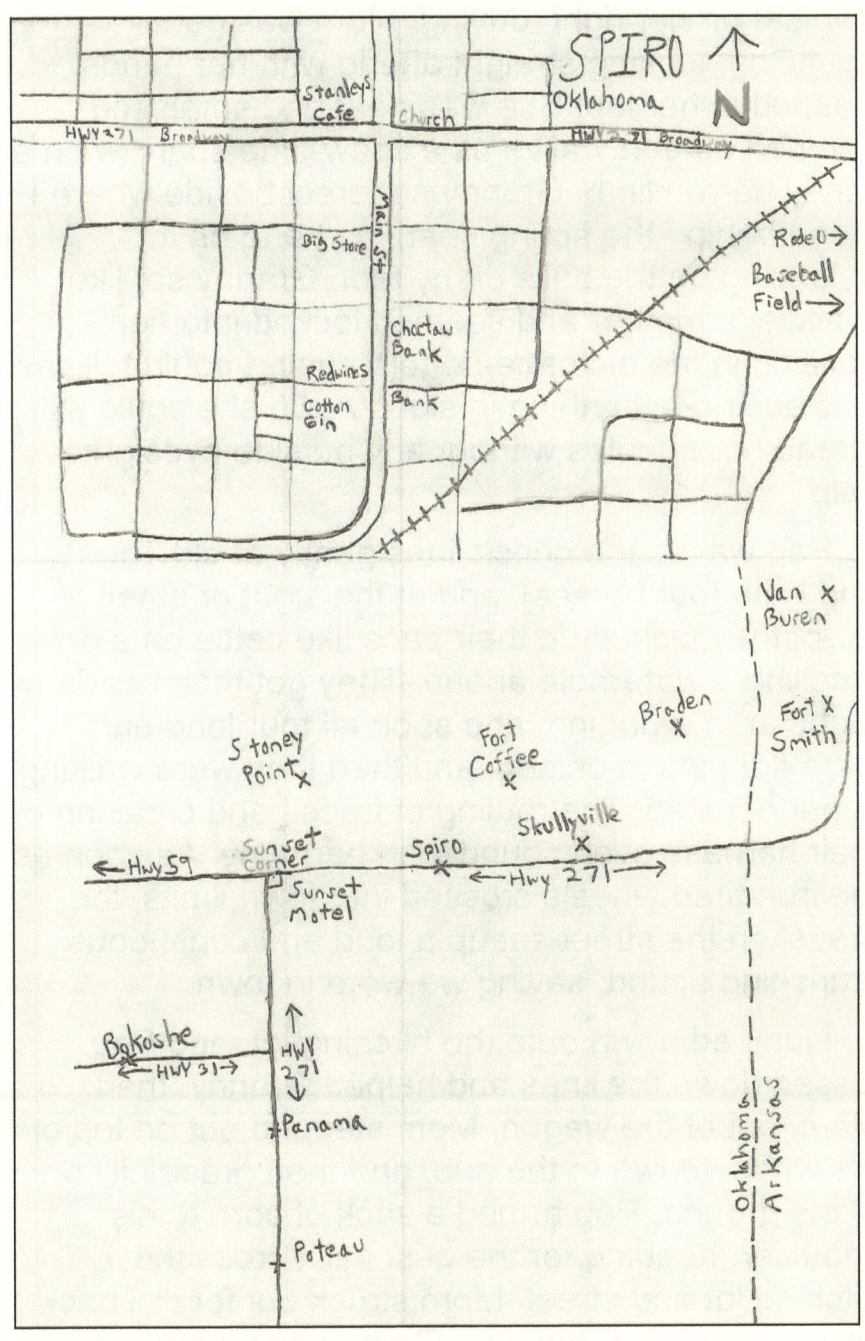

A Day in Spiro, Indian Territory

Mom sat primly in the spring seat of the wagon. Pap sat on her right, driving. Mom was gently bouncing, looking straight ahead with her hands clasped in her lap. She was neat and small and perched as pertly alive as a snow-time sparrow on a windy barren limb. Granny sat erect beside where I stood behind the spring seat, my hand on it, balancing on the balls of my feet. Granny sat like Whistler's mother and seemed locked into her position in the old cane-bottom chair. I could tell she was seeing everything in sight. At 85 she could still thread her needles without any outside eyesight help.

Pap waved the check lines gently at old Tobe and Kate [our horses], and at the sight or smell of town, they picked up their pace like cattle on a drive smelling a waterhole ahead. They got their heads together in swinging, and soon all four long ears were flopping in unison, and then they were walking in perfect step. The rattling of traces and creaking of their harness even sounded in harmony. As soon as the iron-tired wheels crossed into town limits, the gravel on the street set up a loud and continuous crunching sound, saying we were in town.

I jumped down onto the hitching lot, and Pap tossed down the lines and helped Granny, then Mom, out of the wagon. Mom stepped out on top of the wheel, down to the hub, and then gracefully on to the ground. Pap armed a sack of corn to his shoulder, heading for the grist mill across the hitching lot and street. Mom struck out for the back door of the store, handing Granny along and not forgetting to tell me what to bring along myself. I turned my attention to unharnessing and took old Tobe and Kate to the water trough where they lip-sucked their fill.

I short-hitched them on either side of the wagon and gave each a block of alfalfa in the back end of the bed. Then, I reached over in the wagon and came over the sideboards with our egg case and Mom's napkin covered butter box. As I went inside, I read the sign over the door, as I had a thousand times, "Dunklin Bros. Spiro, I.T." although Indian Territory had long since become Oklahoma.

Turning the butter and eggs over to Mom, I headed out toward Main Street, where I would begin my day in town. That would include sneakily buying a dime pack of Polo cigarettes and slopping up a couple of goblets of near beer laced with pepper sauce to out the bitter, and then on to the pool hall to watch the older boys shoot. Or even try my hand at flirting with the town girls. Seems the older you get the more pretty girls you had crazy about you when you were 13. – *Mack Stanley*

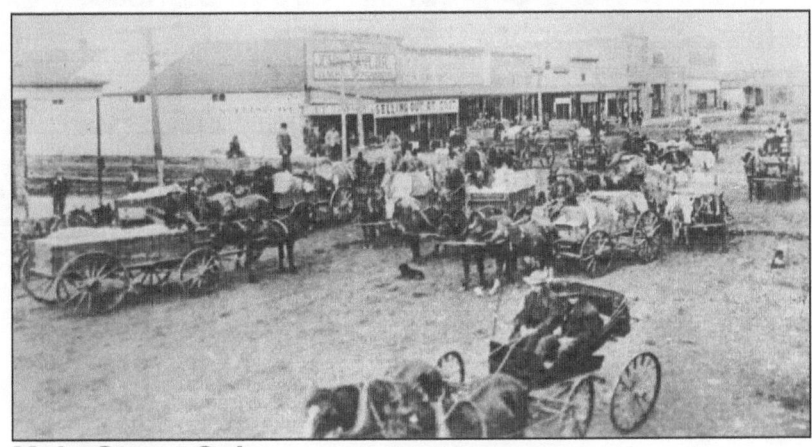

Main Street Spiro

Community Feuds

In times past, some rural communities had feuds that equaled in intensity to those of individuals. Some of the Cache Bottom folks and what they referred to as "Cliff Dwellers" up on Nubbin Ridge didn't geehaw at all. No double harness for them. The "Bottom Ducks," as the uplanders called the lowlanders, thought the upland folks were uppity and the Nubbin Ridgers considered the river-bankers on the level of sharecroppers, which was in fact all you could make of them.

The upland citizens admitted their rocky places were not much, but they were theirs and no landlord could kick them on down the road when the work was all done that fall. The Bottom Ducks allowed they would rather move on twice a year than to spend their lives knocking fire out of the rocks with their bare heels summer after summer.

Both sides were good, people. It was just that they had to have two branches of the same church denomination three miles apart. There was not ever much difference in their financial circumstances. Both sides were so poor there was no use going to town on some Saturdays. Both sides together did not donate many shekels to the coffers of the town merchants, but they all said Sunday wouldn't feel right without butter and egg day in town the day before. When these two factions met in town, it was like a short truce melted them together against the common enemy, the town folks. Both felt their small money was all the town dudes wanted, so they banded together until they crossed town limits again.

They responded to what each other said like a ripe pumpkin lying on the porch. Both sides did a lot of embroidering with their mouths when talking about the other. However, if outsiders bothered either, they banded together. A "I can call them that, but you better not," situation. – *Mack Stanley*

****

When a preacher was put out by either place he passionately declined to accept a church at the other. As one such parson said, "Having been defrocked by Nubbin Ridge, I'd just about accept the worst and go straight on to hell. I wouldn't live in a place that flat if I had to die first. Besides, for 20 years I never preached any harder against the Devil's Domain than I did Cache Bottom."
– *Mack Stanley*

****

We came to get "learnt"

Back pretty close to the turn of the [20th] century, I went to Old Harper School down in the Cache Bottom area for a while. Back then, the kids started to school almost as soon as they no longer had to nurse or wear three cornered pants. They didn't go a full nine months like they do now. We'd get in a couple of months between potato picking time and when the first cotton boils started busting in September. In other words, we went to school when there was nothing important going on, like gathering corn, picking cotton, cutting wood or plowing.

Back then, both boys and girls had to take a whipping when they got out of line. There was a short time there when if a boy was brave enough he could volunteer and take the whipping for a girl. But if it was a man teacher instead of a woman, very few boys were heroic enough to take the laying on of the strap to save a girl. There's a limit to what a big husky boy can do to impress a girl...

If the weather was too bad through the winter, we sometimes got in four months. Winters were long sieges of croupy throats and runny noses in spite of long handled underwear, high top shoes and old thick mackinaws. About half the kids wore strings around their necks with a gob of asafetida tied to them. It wasn't too bad most of the times, but when one of those kids came in damp from snow or sleet and stood too close to the big rosy sided wood stove, whew!

Odor was so bad you wouldn't have been able to smell garlic or onions. Cousin Larnce wore one of those strings. Finally, the teacher sent a note to Uncle Oscar and Aunt Hannah, telling them to make Larnce take a bath next weekend. Hannah wrote back to Miss Prissy and told her they sent Larnce to school to be "learnt, not smelt".

One time, the teacher put little short sentences on the blackboard. Things like "Eyes see." "Noses smell." "Feet run." Little Bill said he guessed he had been put together wrong, as his "feet smelt and his nose run." – *Mack Stanley*

****

Breaking The Fall

In my first days of school at Old Harbor up in Cache Bottom (pronounced Casher), there was no such thing as an automobile parked in the schoolyard. Our landlord was the only man in the area with a car, and they had to dig out a couple of stumps before they could get his Oakland up the lane to his house. One family of kids came in an old buggy, and there were always several saddle ponies hitched under the big oak west of the school. I guess you could have called us a horse-oriented society. Everyone rode horses, from young ladies on their side saddles to men working cattle to boys practicing as future rodeo performers. Even grandparents rode horses.

A new woman teacher came to Old Harper and soon became acquainted with most of the families of the pupils. On a visit to Uncle Oscar's house, this young lady was greeted by all, and found to her surprise that Larnce and Gertie had a younger brother named Arthur whom she had never heard of. Arthur was about ready to begin first year at school, and the teacher found him a bright and lovable youngster.

"Why have you and Hannah never told me anything about your brother Arthur?"

"Well, it's this way, Miss Greenwood," said Larnce, "we don't talk much about him. Arthur fell off of a horse one time." – *Mack Stanley*

****

Mack Stanley has been looking back a few years to his classroom days. "I remember," he says, "I got my best marks in school from my visits to the principal's office."

****

Teachers have come a long way

Here is a copy of a 1918 Oklahoma teacher contract:

This is an agreement between Miss _____, teacher, and the Board of Education of _____ school, whereby Miss _____ agrees to teach in the _____ school for a period of eight months, beginning September 1, 1918. The Board of Education agrees to pay Miss _____ the sum of $75.00 per month.

Miss _____ agrees:

1. Not to get married. This contract becomes null and void immediately if the teacher marries.

2. Not to keep company with men.

3. To be home between the hours of 8 p.m. and 6 a.m. unless in attendance at a school function.

4. Not to loiter downtown in ice cream stores.

5. Not to leave town at any time without permission of the Chairman of the Board of Trusties.

6. Not to smoke cigarettes.

7. Not to drink beer, wine, or whiskey.

8. Not to ride in carriage or automobile with any man other than brother or father.

9. Not to dress in bright colors.

10.   Not to dye hair.

11.   To wear at least two petticoats.

12.   Not to wear dresses more than two inches above the ankles.

13.   To keep the schoolroom clean. To
sweep the classroom at least once a day. To
scrub the classroom floor every week. To
clean the blackboard once a day. To start at
7:00 so the room will be warm when the
children come at 8:00.

Not to use face powder, mascara or paint her
lips. This contract becomes null and void
immediately if the teacher uses face powder
mascara or paints her lips. – *Mack Stanley*

****

Paycheck Not Much

Back in the 1960s the old art teacher Willard
Perry got his paycheck from the principal during our
class period. We all said, "He's a rich man now." Mr.
Perry corrected the notion that he was getting rich
teaching art in the public school system. His
monthly check was a whole $400. Most public
school teachers didn't make much more than
$4,000 to $6,000 per year back then.

Ole Mr. Perry made some impressions on our
class, three of those students turned out to be
professional artists in painting, sculpturing and one
actually became an art teacher.

I remember Oklahoma teachers got ready to go
on strike in 1965 in protest for higher pay. Henry
Belmon was governor in 1965, and again in 1989
when teachers threatened to go on strike for higher
pay and more funding to public education.
– *John Clark*

****

Fists fly for Arkie

A family moved from Ozark Mountains region of Arkansas to Oklahoma. There was a father the mother and an only eight-year-old daughter. The mother had just enough refinement to be a snob.

Before the eight-year-old girl left for school on her first day there, the mother sat the girl down and gave her a good talk. She instructed the daughter to remain aloof from the hillbillies. She informed her that they were riffraff, uncouth, and told her to not get mixed up with them, that she was much better than the Okies.

Every day after school, the daughter came home and told her mother that the boys were always fighting.

The mother humphed her disapproval. "That's disgusting. They are ruffians."

After a couple of weeks, the eight-year-old daughter came in and announced there had been seven fights among the boys that day.

"Well, that's awful," said the mother "What in the world do the brats find to fight so much about anyway?"

"Why, Mama," the daughter said with a touch of pride in her voice, "I thought you knew. They were fighting over me!" – *Mack Stanley*

****

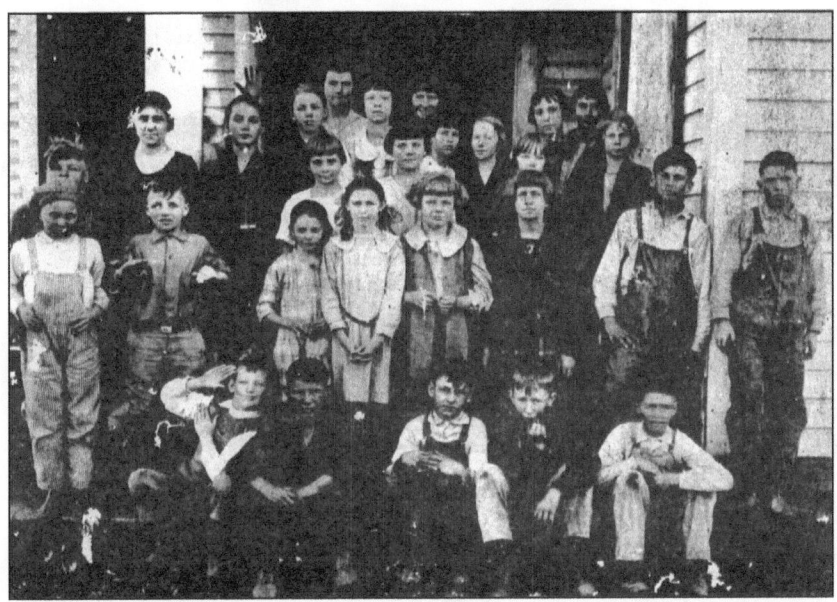

Class of 1923

Cousin Clem Was No Match For Miss Sally

Schools didn't have such things as Kindergarten and Head-Start when Cousin Clemson went to Lone Dove School up in Cache Bottom. Clem was lucky enough to be excused from the cotton patch at six years of age, but he failed every semester through the 8th grade. By that time he was 22, six feet tall and weighed in at 192 pounds.

Miss Sally-Lee Thomas had been the teacher for a long time out there. She was not little in stature, and not really big either, but she was strong and wiry and had all the quick motions of a cricket near a hornet's nest. We kids wouldn't have known the word 'psychic' from 'psoriasis,' if we had met it out on the big road, but that was what Sally-Lee Thomas must have been. She could be monitoring out on one side, just in time to catch some big Choctaw boy commit some heinous crime against an innocent victim. She marched stiff-legged around to face the culprit and herded him toward the wood shed, and closed the door behind her.

Throughout the years Miss Sally-Lee Thomas must have switched old Clemson half a hundred times. This had no adverse affect on him. In fact our cousin actually thought he was in love with Miss Sally-Lee.

After the diplomas were passed out for the 8th grade, Clemson maneuvered Miss Sally off to one side and began to tell her how he felt. She took him by the hand and led him toward the wood shed. This encounter was a rendition of what had happened many times before. When they came back out, Miss Sally said, "Young man, you get crazy ideas like that out of your head, and keep this in mind: I never met a boy too big for me to whip!"

– *Mack Stanley*

****

Respect School Officials, From Janitor On Up

It is a wonder that kids of my era (circa 1900 Indian Territory) ever survived their juvenility and still stayed together all in one piece. We were completely surrounded by the enemy. That included anyone more than 20 years old of either sex. Over that age all were categorized as adversary. Our primary disadvantage was that from diaper age through elementary school we had absolutely no organization among our own ranks. We went about trying to stand up against this forceful opposition in a very ragtag manner. We couldn't even estimate their superior forces. We only knew we were vastly outnumbered. It was almost like we were dumb clucks and couldn't see, and they had eyes in the back of their heads.

All we had to do in school was to step one-inch out of line and we had everyone from the superintendent, principal, to our teachers, on our case. Our Miss Romine was very good at that. Younger Miss Prather was much harder to agitate to the point of explosiveness but then she'd go around with you.

Last, but not least, was Miss Savage, who sometimes seemed to glory in trying to live up to her name. This browbeating of us ran the gamut down even to Mr. Wilson, the janitor. If Mr. Wilson ever jumped you out, you were in a mess of trouble. We kids loved Mr. Wilson, it was outrageous how we curried and catered for his favor. Most of us seemed to think he could walk on water. To fall beneath his smiling attention was compared worse than absolute banishment would be from other mortals. Contrary to many of our higher paid educators, this white headed custodian was looked up to with great respect. If he failed to stop sweeping or carrying out trash when you passed and looked fiercely at you under those shaggy and bushy eyebrows and muttered, "You done wrong," you knew you were in his doghouse for a week. – *Mack Stanley*

****

Cousin Dave Went Over The Fence

Ole Cousin Dave was always in trouble of some sort back in high school during the mid-1960s.

Dave was a 'good ole boy' but he did it just a little too close to the house one too many times and finally got caught in the act.

I can't remember what he actually did or got caught doing, but it was something serious enough to get him sent off to military school for strict discipline.

Cousin Dave got sent up to Oklahoma Military Academy in Claremore. I'm sure this is one place Dave never planned on visiting in his lifetime.

The old military retired drill sergeants and officers feast on youths who disrupt society and protest against the system.

Cousin Dave didn't like this situation from the get-go. He had to find a way to get out of this military institution with a wrought iron fence surrounding the campus. Dave was tall, slim guy with some experience in the sport of track and field.

We really didn't think old Dave was coming back until he graduated from the military school.

Well, a few days later, old Cousin Dave showed up in class at Tahlequah High School as if nothing ever happened.

I got to inquiring about how Dave got out of the military academy so quick. I asked him point blank — "Dave, how did you get out of that military complex with fences all around the campus?"

Dave looked around the classroom with a big smile on his face and simply said: "I pole vaulted over the fence" — I just couldn't believe something like that really happened. Forty years later, I asked the same question and got the same answer. He really did pole vault over the fence.

He waited till after dark, walked out of the barracks to the track field, picked up the pole used by the pole vaulters and promptly vaulted over the 10-foot (or was it a 6-foot?) fence in front of the Will Rogers Memorial and escaped from the dreaded military academy.

Cousin Dave called his girlfriend Twyla in Tahlequah to come pick him up and take him back home. – *John Clark*

****

My Uncle Oscar

He's nice when he's sober, but when he drinks too much he gets obnoxious. You might say Ossie is a gentleman…up to a pint. He once told me about the happiest weekend of his life. It began with him in the men's room unnoticed when they locked the liquor store late Saturday. – *Mack Stanley*

****

Uncle Os & Aunt Hanny Good Kinfolk

I guess you could say we were too poor to paint and too proud to whitewash. Anything in between was seldom considered. Uncle Oscar never let you forget that he was poor (and stingy). Any time on a visit to his and Hannah's house, when he gave me three .410 shotgun shells in the morning of a rabbit hunt, he let it be know he expected three cottontails in exchange. He also insisted that they be fat, no skin and bones stuff. He pointed out that a spry sprout like myself could probably even catch a rabbit before wasting a shell. Ossie always intended to have his tongue in cheek when he said things like this, but I knew better than to waste one of his shells while I was an invited guest in his household.

I had to agree with all their other nephews and nieces though, that they were better received at this house than any other of our relatives. At least they didn't throw rocks at us when they saw us coming. They actually came out on the porch and recognized you instead of making unwelcoming remarks like, "Whose place are you looking for," and "Am I supposed to know you?" and "Let's see now, you are one of Cousin Willie's boys I believe. Well, come on up on the porch anyway."

Long before supper time one of those elder relatives would inquire, "How long do you intend to be with us this time?" and things to scare you off like, "If you stay till Monday we start chopping cotton and I got a hoe that will just fit your hands."

Most of those visits were during that period when Aunt Hannah had to be doing something all the time. To her way of thinking, time was money and she did not intend to waste a penny. There was some workaholic in Hannah, though we hadn't even heard the word alcoholic up to that time. We always said, "He's a drunk". One bad winter spell when the wind was howling and snow as banked up to the windows, she ran completely out of anything to do. She became so nervous Os would have had her put away if he could have got to town. That was the time when she unraveled a crocheted shawl and did it all over again just for some work to do. When her needles were clacking industriously it was no time to bother Hannah. We kids knew she would box our ears if we pestered her at all. That was the same spell when the men folks wore all the spots off the dominoes and the pitch cards were so frazzled you couldn't tell a queen from a king. – *Mack Stanley*

****

The Best Holiday Ever

At least a couple of times a year, Hannah catches Oscar completely forgetting one sort of an anniversary or the other. At breakfast one morning, our aunt leaned over to Oscar and coyly said, "Know what day this is Ossie?" He didn't know, but he was not about to be caught that easily. He said, "Why of course I do dear, you didn't think I'd forget today, did you? Here's one hundred dollars, I want you to go out and buy yourself a new sexy dress, and tonight, I'm taking you to the fanciest restaurant in town. Then later, we will go on to that new night spot and dance until the wee hours. She said, "Oh, thank you."

They went to the most expensive cafe in town and enjoyed the best entree on the menu, then on to the first-class night club and almost danced the night away.

Much later, when they were driving home just before dawn, she snuggled up close and laid her head on his shoulder.

After several minutes, Oscar finally broke the blissful silence with, "Well, Honey Bunch, did today live up to your expectations? Was it everything you hoped it would be?"

"Oh yes, darling," she sighed, then cooed into his ear, "Even better, it was the very best Ground Hog Day I ever spent." – *Mack Stanley*

****

Good Neighbor

Aunt Hannah and Uncle Oscar had a three-day squabble due to her trying to do her fall cleaning with Uncle Oscar in her way every which way she turned. He claimed she was nagging him. Finally, he moved out into the little tool shed on the back of the lot. He kept on mowing the lawn and was still keeping the garden hoed out. Every day brought him out a bowl of stew, a couple of sandwiches, a salad, or a piece of pie.

Cousin Larnce had seen for some time what was going on, and he said to Uncle Oscar, "Why don't you move completely away somewhere. She's impossible!"

"Oh, I don't know," reasoned Uncle Oscar, "She makes a pretty good neighbor." – *Mack Stanley*

****

The First Radio

When radio first came to our little town of Spiro, most of us were initiated to Lum and Abner and Amos and Andy at Jim Ed Carter's little service station. Most of us just called it 'the filling station.' Uncle Oscar was about the fourth man in town to jump out on a limb and buy one of these contraptions that few knew anything about. As was usual with Ossie, he made a production and holiday of the occasion.

Bryan Forbes, considered a genius in some instances, brought the radio out one Saturday morning and spent two hours putting up the antenna and making hookups with batteries. Bryan put the radio right where Oscar wanted it, right on the front porch, where everyone up and down Main Street could see and hear it. The radio playing was to start at 10 A.M. The crowd began to gather at 7. By starting time, our uncle's yard was filled to overflowing and back out into the street, making it hard for dray wagons, buggies and automobiles to get through down toward the depot.

At exactly 10 A.M., Uncle Oscar and Bryan came out together and the young man showed Uncle Oscar which button to twist. Great balls of music came out. The fascinated onlookers crowded forth, forward tearing the gate off its hinges into the yard and onto the little rickety front porch, all for a closer look. Push turned to shove as the near hysterical folks clambered together like a soccer team gone mad.

The little porch couldn't take it. A mass of humanity packed every square foot floor space, until the whole thing caved in and brought an end to the wireless demonstration. People were standing up to their hips in shattered porch.

On his was home Dick Webb ran his Model T off a high bank into the City Lake. Old Doc Crawford said Dick must have been woolgathering about the mysteries of the new fangled radio! – *Mack Stanley*

****

Just draw one on me

A specialty salesman was calling on a company store over at Poker Bend in Oklahoma. He struck up a conversation with the storekeeper and in course of the talking the salesman mentioned that he had just sold an order of goods to Oscar Stanley over at Short Mountain.

Uncle Charlie, who was holding down one end of the bench in front of the pot bellied coal stove overheard the man, and after they were finished talking, Charlie said to the salesman, "So you know Oscar Stanley do you?"

"Yes sir I do. Do you know Oscar? "

"Guess I do, Mister. He's my oldest brother. How's old Ossie doing these days?"

"He's doing fine…has a pretty fair trade in his store, a section of good bottom land and 300 head of whiteface. Yes, you could say Oscar is fine."

"Well, sir, if you see him this trip, I wish you'd tell him his brother Charlie is mighty hard up. My cotton failed this year, and my corn all turned to nubbins, and the bank down at the county seat is foreclosing my mortgage. Looks like I'm a plumb goner. Tell Oscar if he's ever going to help me, there will never be a better time than right now."

They walked out to the salesman's car, and he asked Charlie if he ever took a drink. Charlie admitted that he did, so they sat in the man's car and had a drink. Then they had another. "So, you know my brother Oscar. If you see him, tell him I'm getting by tolerably well." They sat in the car and had a couple more. Then Charlie said, "If you do see old Oscar, you tell him I'm getting along first-rate and making a good living."

They talked of other matters, and in the course of an hour had several more drinks. Came time for Charlie to start home, and he got out and stood by the car. He said to the salesman, "Say, about my brother Oscar. You tell him if he ever needs any money, just draw a draft on me!" – *Mack Stanley*

****

Uncle Charlie, Becomes Just Charlie

It took me a long time to catch up with Uncle Charlie. He was Mama's baby brother and that was good enough for me. Besides, when I was little every time he came, he brought me a couple of Uncle Sam's Kisses (cost a penny each) and that was my favorite store-bought confection. And he always told a funny story also. From snatches of hushed conversations I finally heard enough to tell me Charlie wouldn't do. I couldn't figure that out exactly. He seemed such a jolly fellow, while a couple of other uncles were such sourpuss characters. The fact that Uncle Charlie was apt to go hunting or fishing when his cotton needed laying-by, and other stories like that were broadcast among the neighbors without reserve.

But still I had to learn the hard way, I was about 10 when he came by in his old Ford pickup and asked if I wanted to go to Fort Smith with him. At first, Mama was not in favor, but I guess the way I showed out with such a fit to go is what made her give in.

Mama took me in the side room and warned: "You work hard for your money, so don't give Charles any money (she was the only one who ever called him Charles). He won't pay you back." I said I wouldn't give him any money.

It took most of the rest of the day to wind up near the Union Depot on Rogers Avenue. The roads were muddy and the old section-line route zig zagged this way and that way through Old Town, by Ainsworth's Spring, Murray Spur, Braden, Peno and finally over the little Iron bridge across the Poteau River, through Coke Hill and downtown to the big union railroad station in Fort Smith.

There was a rooming house upstairs across Rogers. Uncle Charlie was not bashful, he said: "Well Sprout, since I furnished transportation, how's about you springing for the room rent? The rates are .50¢ single and .75¢ double." Forgetting I was invited, I figured that would ok. I was too excited at seeing that wonderful Union Station to remember Mama's cautioning. That was the biggest place I had ever seen. The rounded dome in the front part reached halfway to the sky and the waiting corridor and covered-over loading and unloading area seemed to run halfway back out to Coke Hill,

We ate a liver and onion supper at Jim's Eat Place .15¢ each, and then we went to the Imp Theater .50¢ and Uncle Charlie suggested we go Dutch. Suited me. I thought I was getting off light for the time of my life!

Two weeks later Uncle Charlie came by. He said he was on his way to Little Rock to get his brother out of jail. Mama was not at home, so I fell for it and loaned him the only five dollars I had. He never paid me back. From that day forward he became just plain old Charlie.

In my little Day Book I wrote, "Old Charlie owes me five dollars!" – *Mack Stanley*

****

Uncle Charlie and Aunt Millicent

At the least provocation, Uncle Charlie and his wife Millicent over at Poker Bend, Oklahoma can have a few hundred words at each other. Their vocalizing may range from mildly cantankerous to blatantly irate. They are our fussin' kinfolk. Aunt Millie says Charlie's disposition would sometimes maker Jack the Ripper seem like Caspar Milquetoast. Charlie then compares her with Carrie Nation with two hatchets. Millie says she would rather kiss Khadafy than shake hands with Charlie after one of their rages.

Millie says he is as stingy as the Chicago Bears defense and as tight as the outside of a scaly-bark hickory nut tree. It took her a long time to get around to calling him by his first name. All those four letter words kept getting in the way. "If he gave you the key to the city," she often says, "it wouldn't open anything but the jail." "He still wouldn't be my type," she goes on to say, "if I had to have a transfusion and he was the only donor." Millie offered to go hunting with Charlie until he insisted she wear his old brown overcoat and coonskin cap.

She claimed that garb made her look like something anyone would take a pot shot at.

While examining her, Old Doc Crawford asked if she woke up cranky in the morning. She said, "No, I let old Cranky sleep. That way I don't have to listen to him at breakfast." Millie can read old Charlie like a book. She says he's about as exciting as McGuffey's First Reader. She can read him quicker than the label on a can of beans.

Charlie said at first he thought she was shrinking violet. The word was "Shrieking." Millie says she is going to try her best to get a birth certificate. She needs proof he is alive. – *Mack Stanley*

****

Too Many Pocket Knives

Someone once said Oscar was small for his site. He was 5'2" and weighed in at 110 pounds if you didn't take any off for a heavy dew. He thought he was a tough nut (he was a nut all right).

The way he boasted to Little Sister and myself, included statements like, "I'm one hundred and ten pounds of walking hell! Anybody who calls me out has done jumped up a scorpion."

In his younger years he liked to go for a late supper at the Wide Awake Cafe in the 500 block on Garrison Ave. over in Fort Smith, Arkansas. This was the "in" place for the fast crowd of that day. One New Years Eve when he was there the place was filled with clattering and chattering diner although it was around midnight.

A beautifully dressed good-looking middle aged woman came in the front door and surveyed the noisy crowd. She looked disappointed that all the tables were taken. Oscar had his waiter tell the lady she could share his table if she liked. She agreed thankfully and sat with him. Although our uncle was only about 20 at the time and the lady was a well-preserved woman of 40, they got along splendidly. This fine looking woman said she lived only three blocks north on Sixth St., and invited him to walk her home. Once there she invited him in for a cocktail.

After talking for an hour, the lady said, "You're welcome to stay overnight if you wish. I have another bedroom. Oscar couldn't help but grin to himself.

Next morning as Oscar was about to leave he said, I feel like I've imposed on you, I hope to see you again, is there some way I can repay your hospitality?"

"No no, I don't need a thing," she halted her speech, and then continued,"Oh yes, there is one thing. Do you carry a pocket knife?"

"Oh sure, I always carry a good Barlow."

"Well, you just drop the knife you have in the left hand drawer in that dresser over there.

Oscar did as instructed, and saw instantly that drawer was almost filled with an assortment of pocket knives. "What in the world are you hoarding all these pocket knives for?"

"Well, I'll tell you," she said, "Right now I'm still good looking and can get almost any young man I want. But one of these days I'll become old and not be so desirable." Then she smiled as if to herself and said, "And we all know that a boy will do almost anything for a good pocket knife." – *Mack Stanley*

****

K.C.&S. Caused Baby Boom in Mid-20's

Back in the mid-twenties we had a population explosion in our little town of Spiro. Old Doc Crawford, who sort of kept tabs on things like that couldn't figure out the cause. He asked some of the smart men about town, like Harvey Bryan, Ree V. Smith, and Lee Smith for opinions on what may have caused it. None of them were any help.

Uncle Oscar stopped Doc on Main Street and said, "Doc, I bet Granny Loudermilk knows why it happened."

Granny Loudermilk was judged to be about 100 years old, and somewhat of a recluse who lived in her little two-roomed house out near the new school buildings.

Old Doc was willing to try anything, he pulled up in front of the small house in his high-top little Ford Coupe. He climbed out and went through the lopsided gate into Granny's yard. It was hard-packed earth with not a weed nor sprig of grass, clean as a pin. It evidently had just been swept with a brush broom.

Granny was sitting on her porch, where she spent much of her fair-weather time. She always wore a Gingham dress and "poke" bonnet.

Doc was a little ill at ease, when he said, "I'm Doctor Crawford."

Granny perked up with: "I know who you are Doctor. I've seen you pass here a thousand times in your little Doctor's Special Ford, I never have ridden in one of those yet."

Now Doc got right to the point. "I was wondering if you could tell me why there's been so many new babies born here in the last two or three years."

"Oh sure Doctor, my niece explained that all to me. She said three years ago that The Kansas City Southern Railroad put on that new crack passenger train. It comes through here about 10 minutes to four A.M., like a bat out of the hot place. It makes so much noise blowing that whistle, it wakes everybody up. My niece says she guesses there are a lot of other men her like her old man. It's too early to get up and too late to go back to sleep. And they are too nervous to lay there and do nothing until gettin' up time."

It was all clear to Doc now, so he thanked Granny. As he turned to leave Granny said, "I sure would love to take a ride in that little coupe of yours."

Old Doc said, "How about now?"

Granny said, "That's mighty fine with me."

– *Mack Stanley*

****

Running Away From Home

I guess one of the first things I learned about was the power of my threat to run away from home, over my young mother.

Mama was less than 17 years old when I came along. When I was eight, I thought I was the king and Mama was my older slave. She was too afraid I might actually run away from home.

I heard one of her neighbors chastise her with: "You're spoiling that kid rotten. You treat him like he was somebody. You carry him around on a stick." I didn't know what that last meant, but I sensed disapproval from Mama's friend. I never liked that woman any more.

Then, it came about that Mama changed one day: When next I indicated I would flee the nest and go down in Texas and pick cotton with Uncle Oscar if I did not get my way. Mama showed no concern.

Always before, she had brought forth offers of my favorite molasses cake and sweet milk to change my mind. This time however, Mama went to the woodpile and chose a slim stick about three feet long. I had a sudden horror that she was going to tan my hide. She never had.

She then went to the kitchen table and spread one of Papa's big red bandannas out and put sandwiches and fruit on it. Then, she gathered up the corners and tied them together and stuck one end of the stick through the knots. She put my coat on me and my cap on my head and placed the stick across my shoulder hobo style and pushed me out the door with a hard slap across my backside.

"Now, that's the way to run away from home," seemed to be her parting words.

Fifty yards down the small lane that led to the Big Road, I turned and looked back expecting to see Mama coming after me or motioning for me to return. Instead, she was already busy in the yard firing up the big black pot for the weekly wash.

I was too far to turn back, so I went on to the high board gate and climbed up intending to go on over down to the county road. But I could not force myself to go on down on the outside.

I perched on top of that gate and watched a stream of cotton wagons go by. One line going toward town was loaded with cotton and the reserve parade were on their way home empty. I tried not to look toward the house every three minutes but failed.

Each time, I saw Mama working furiously at her rub-board and poking the clothes in the hot water. It seemed like she was talking to herself and she sneaked a look my way now and then. I wished she'd call me. I starved out long before noon and ate all the food in the bandanna. I was very sleepy after dinner and the only thing that kept me awake was the precarious perch on the hard top of the gate and the fear of falling down in under one of those cotton wagons.

I kept an Eagle eye in the direction of the house for any sign from Mama, but she was too busy with her all day washing to call me back.

Boy! Was I tuckered out. After a lifetime atop that hateful gate, the shadows from the trees began to lengthen and I gave up, climbed back down inside and went back up the lane dragging my stick and empty bandanna.

When I neared the house, Mama spied me and swooped down the lane with her dress tail and bonnet strings flying out behind. She was leaning partly forward to scoop me up in her arms.

Then she went into her play-act of pretense that we often did: "Oh, my goodness," she said tearfully, "here is my son who has been gone to Texas for such a long time. My! How you have grown. Your Daddy will be so pleased that you've come home at last. He has missed you a lot."

We were blubbering cheek to cheek and it was hard to tell which one was the biggest kid. "Oh, I do so hope you never run away again," Mama said.

My answer was, "Oh, I never will Mama." And I never did. – *Mack Stanley*

****

K.C.&S. No Fun

Uncle Oscar and Aunt Hannah had only one son after Cousin Larnce. Aunt Hanah was later heard to say, "I should have quit while I was ahead." The name adopted for this new man child was K.C.&S. Of course, that was his given name, not the surname. They gave him that moniker because the first things the baby seemed to be aware of were the railroad trains running by their house.

The railroad was the Kansas City and Southern, usually abbreviated to K.C.&S. The passing trains were the only things K.C.&S. paid any attention to all through his three-cornered pants days. He always seemed to be listening for them with some air of stilled expectancy.

We thought he was never going to talk, but right away at an early age he could imitate any noise made by the trains going by day or night. Soon he was telling time by them also.

When the "Cuckle Burr Bunch" came along with their "dinky" make-up coal train switching around the neighborhood, K.C.&S. knew it was time for his nap. He ate, went to bed, and got up in the morning by the whistling and roaring of the trains. When the West Bound came through at 4 a.m. K.C.&S. decided it was time for all to rise and shine.

Uncle Oscar said it was too early to get up, K.C.&S. intimated it was too late to go back to sleep, and he always won out. No wonder.

Times like that was when he began to blow his lonesome highballs and went on for an hour. Imagine listening to him go on! He began whistling lonesome, like he was about to cross Coal Creek three miles down the tracks. Next he whistled like he was at a crossing only one mile away. Soon, came a thundering imperiling explosion that rattled the windows, as he imitated passing the house. Then the sound seemed to pass and begin to diminish in road, but he added a clackety clack noise like the train has passed and was going away clicking over the cross times.

Eventually you were not sure you heard that last fading lonesome whistle. Was it just a memory? K.C.&S. kept repeating this routine until everyone get up. As K.C.&S. grew up he let it be known that he was going to be a railroad man. Hardly anyone was surprised when at seventeen he joined the railroad at his first opportunity. Not with his beloved Kansas City & Southern, but as a tryout on the Fort Smith & Western to Oklahoma City (F.S.&W.).

He quit. Back home he said, "I'd rather just stay home and listen to K.C.&S. than work on the old Foot Sore & Weary." – *Mack Stanley*

****

I remember way back when I was a cocky teenager. I used to ride the Fort Smith & Western quite a bit between Spiro and Fort Smith, Arkansas. I began to notice that every time we went through the town of Braden, a pretty girl came out on the porch and waved at me. Finally, I thought I might be missing something, so I brashly went over there to see just who she was. It turned out she wasn't waving at me after all. Her father was the brakeman. – *Mack Stanley*

****

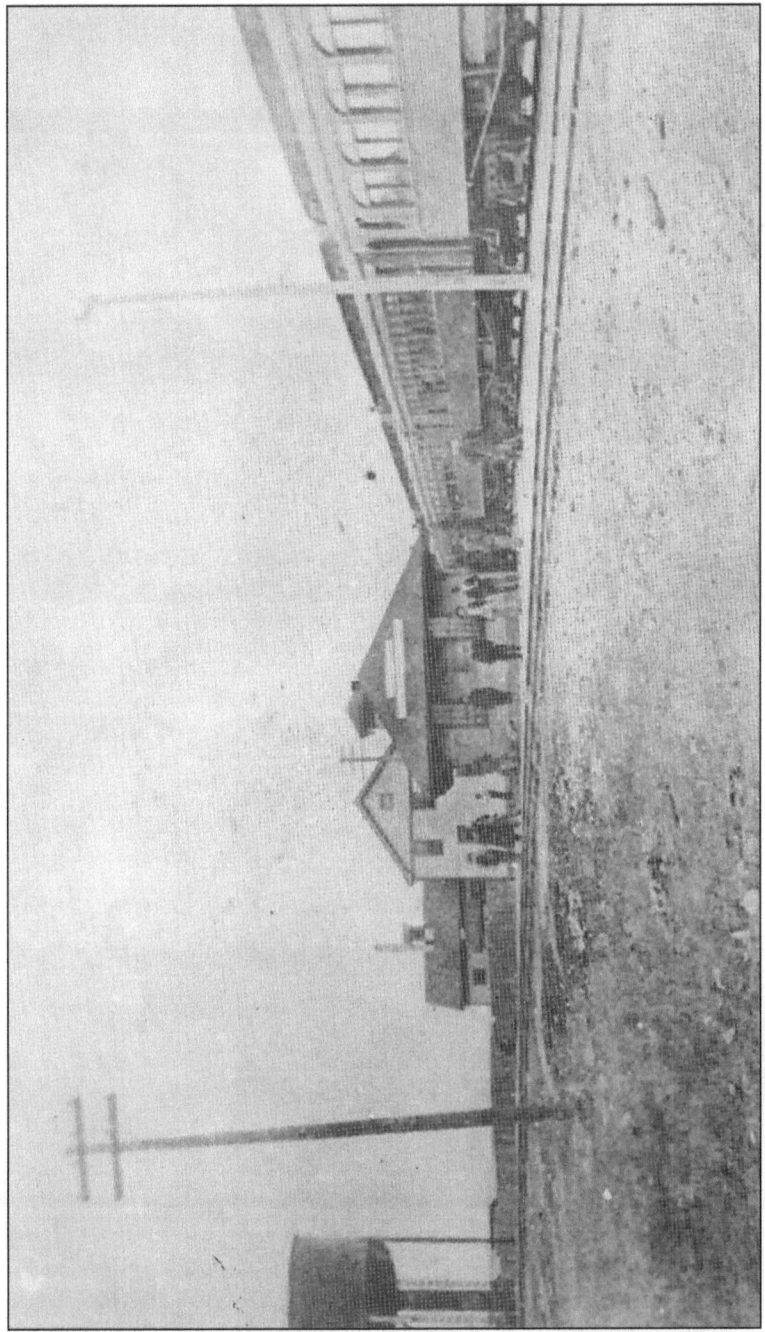

Old K.C.&S. depot at South end of Main St. Spiro

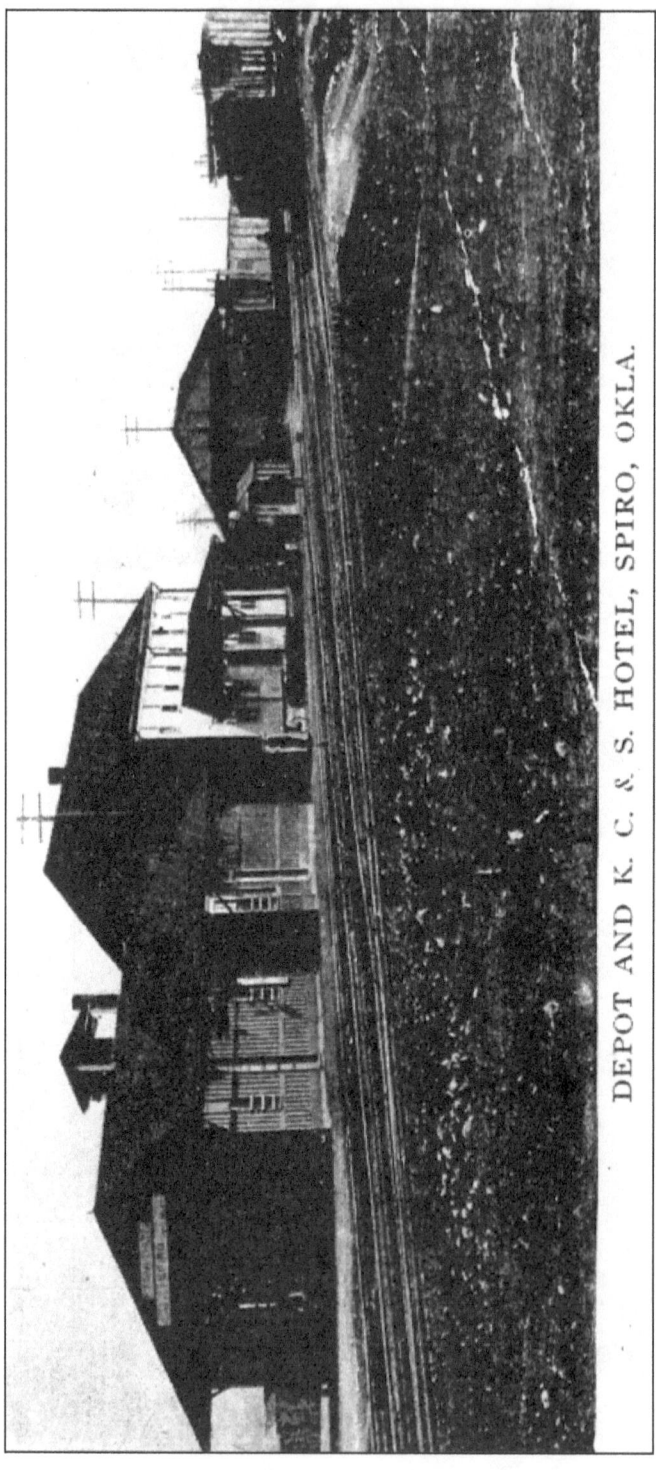

DEPOT AND K. C. & S. HOTEL, SPIRO, OKLA.

Kansas City and Southwestern Depot

This was the second depot at Spiro. The first was a boxcar put off beside the track down by the old underpass on old Highway # 271, although the underpass nor highway were there yet. The third depot was a most attractive brick building. The pictured depot was torn down or moved away as was the Kansas City Southern Hotel. The building on the right remained for years to come and finally became known as "The Potato Shed." At one time Spiro shipped out more potatoes than any town on the K.C.&S. – *Mack Stanley*

****

What a man really needs

A while after Uncle Oscar moved from Tulsa back to his old home town a neighbor asked "how does it feel to be in a small town again?"

"It wasn't easy for a while," Oscar responded. "To tell you the truth I didn't think I'd make it until I got me a paramour (which the dictionary says is an 'illicit lover'). That made a world of difference."

"A paramour? Does your wife know? Doesn't she care?" the neighbor queried.

Of Course she knows. And why should she mind? She doesn't care how I cut my grass," Oscar explained...– *Mack Stanley*

****

Cousin Larnce

Two of Aunt Hannah's kids were having a knock down drag out in the front yard. A passing stranger stopped and watched with amusement.

"Aren't they something?" he said.

"They surely are. Sometimes I wish I had six of them," Hannah mused.

"How many have you?" the stranger asked.

"Twelve," Hannah answered wearily.
– *Mack Stanley*

****

When Cousin Larnce was a small boy, he asked his mother where he came from.

That was a little too sudden for Aunt Hannah. She stammered and sputtered and made funny noises and said "you better ask your father."

When Oscar came in from the field his small son asked "papa, where did I come from?"

The question left Oscar even less prepared. He walked out behind the barn with Larnce but couldn't get started on the answer. He fidgeted, took off his coat, rolled up his sleeves, wiped his brow, stuttered and coughed and finally gulped "Larnce, why did you ask me that question?"

With all the innocence of a six-year-old Larnce explained, "Little Bill said he came from Missouri and he wanted to know where I came from."
– *Mack Stanley*

****

As a small boy, Cousin Larnce went crying to his mother "all the kids make fun of me. They say I have a big head."

Aunt Hannah, a loving mother said "don't listen to them. They're only jealous. Your pretty head is not too big. Now dry your tears and run to the store for mother. Get me 25 pounds of potatoes."

"Where's the shopping bag? Larnce asked.

"We don't have one. Use your hat," Hannah replied. – *Mack Stanley*

****

Rainy Days Were Haircuttin' Days

Rainy days on the farm were times for catching up on special jobs around the place. One of those bad-day tasks was group-haircutting. Uncle Charley's brood numbered a baker's dozen with boys in a two-third majority. Charley had a pretty good days work laid out, come the haircutting day. For these occasions he had two different sized lard buckets to fit all heads. They went down over the head like a tin stocking cap. The results were what we called 'round haircuts'. The father said this plan worked out well until they came to Clemson. It took a water bucket for him. Other chores included sharpening of all cutting tools, like axes, saws, butcher knives and such. Other rainy day jobs were like greasing all the axles of moving equipment.

This father and son duo had recently devised a funny pattern of talking semi- tongue-tied, just for their own amusement, when they were together working on rainy days. They gave a S A T sound and a L A W sound and so on.

One morning Charley and Clemson were greasing the wagon. They had lubed the wheels and decided to give the center pin in the doubletree a good dollop while they were at it. If you have never had experience trying to handle doubletree with two singletrees still attached, you have never known true frustration. This is the most unwieldy combination ever put together by man. Somehow, Charley got his thumb caught in this entanglement and cried out in their special jargon: "Wif it up thos! Wif it up! It dot my fumb taught!"

Clemson cried back at Charley: "I taint wif it Pa, it dot my fumb too!" – *Mack Stanley*

****

Skeeters in Catchum Bottom

When I was a mean little kid and we lived up in Cache Bottom near the Arkansas River, the wild canebrakes covered several square miles and were higher than a man's head on horseback.

Sometimes wolves came up near the back door around where the lamplight shone and tried to share the poochie-gravy and table scraps with our hound-dog. At other times a panther came along close enough to be heard screaming in the night like a tortured woman. Some said that squalling was a decoy to entice a human being out there. I was never brave enough to investigate and try to find out for sure.

But it was not the big wild ferocious animals that dealt us the most trouble in Cache Bottom. It was the small flying objects we knew as "skeeters." They came in darkening clouds, flying in good formation, with their long proboscises sticking out at us. They were ready to zoom or dive bomb and gouge you worse than an oil company with its own credit card. Some were big enough to show upon radar. You had to have on hob-nailed boots before you dared to stomp on the. It took only a few punctures from them to turn you as malaria-yellow as a highway caution sign. When one of those pesky dudes bit you, it felt like you had been vaccinated with a post-hole digger, by a rough horse-doctor.

To survive these pests, we almost wore a trail back and forth to Old Doc's drug store for more "Swamp Root" chill tonic and a little quinine and a little calomel on the side. – *Mack Stanley*

****

On The Farm

As a kid, I was "work brittle" about doing chores when I visited Uncle Oscar on the farm. I loved my "guest status" and exercised and stretched out as long as I could. Aunt Hannah loved to go about her chores, and I sometimes went along on cold evenings which were more than chilly and crisp when snow was on the ground. In the barn, she would hang her lantern on a nail in a center pole, and it cast soft moving shadows until it stopped swinging pendulum- like, creating some small suggestion of warmth in there.

All the cats on the place tagged along to supervise the milking, beggars for a squirt of the warm sweet milk. They were expert at opening their mouths in just the right way to catch the stream. The weaned calves sucked up their share from a bucket, switching their tails in hungry excitement and later rambunctiously kicked over the bucket when it was empty.

There was a moment of church-like atmosphere in the old barn at these times. The untroubled way the "fresh" cow spoke to her newborn calf when it nudged her roughly, and the day-end clucking of the chickens as they went to roost, and the cooing pigeons up among the high rafters, making their lonesome sounds, and the way they sounded like miniature helicopters when they were excited enough to flutter off into the night.

Then when we started back for the house, I was surprised by the full brightness of the moon and all the twinkling stars. Aunt Hannah's old, brakeman-type swinging lantern picked up reflections from the snow like diamonds scattered around. Our old barnyard rubber boots made loud noises crunching the hard-frosted-over snow in the path. We spoiled its clean freshness with the barn floor dirtiness on our boots as we carried the warm milk toward the house.

Old Blue was curious enough to come alive and act like a puppy in the knowledge he would get his saucered share of this nightly treat.

The still-following cats, fastidious to a fault, avoided Blue's boisterous animation for fear (heaven forbid) he might knock some dirty snow on them. They looked on this mere hound with aloof disdain.

ty.

Coming to the kitchen door, it was pleasant to look back toward the dim shadow of the barn across pale expanse of snow and know you were going inside where it was-warn and cheerful, and a good big supper awaited. – *Mack Stanley*

****

S&H Green Stamps for the Rich

Junior Morgan was the same small boy who once told the grouchy old banker it was not good for his business not to give him a complementary bank calendar. "That's a sorry way to get new business," was how Junior put it. Jr. Morgan was a "My Daddy" boy who always had to tag along, he prefaced every statement he made with "My Daddy can..." it would have been hard to convince Junior that his father could not walk on water.

In reality, Bill Morgan the father, was just an avenge guy who had been out of work for six months. He'd had to give up the small house they were buying when he fell behind with payments, it had been nip and tuck with their city bills before that. They were so broke they didn't even have store coupons. Even S&H Green Stamps were scarce around their place. For a while there Junior and his mother had to go and stay with her parents. Bill had to refinance his seven-year old car to keep wheels under himself. He thought there for a while he might have to give up Tuesday night bowling.

Then, when things looked darkest, Bill got called back to work. He figured it would take three years to really get back on their feet and out of this hold of poverty.

Bill had scraped and borrowed to get enough money to have his old car's brakes relined. He had to do this to get back and forth to work. This new unexpected cost would make it slim pickings that much longer at their home.

The man at the garage said it would be one day before Bill could get his car, but let him have an old loaner to go to work one day. Driving home in the old jalopy, Bill noticed that Junior seemed worried about something. When he asked his son what was wrong, Junior said, "Dad, can't we drive the other way to get home? If our neighbors see us coming up in this old wreck, they might think we're poor."
– *Mack Stanley*

****

Traffic Problems in Downtown Spiro

Shortly after Mr. Ford's Tin Lizzie first rolled off the line, "Pa" Duncas, our town marshal, began to have traffic problems on Main St. in Spiro, Oklahoma. Before that, the vehicular movement had been multi-directional, every which way, and slow, since it was only wagons and team, buggies and horsebackers, with little danger involved. The new horseless carriages changed all of that.

The town council thought they had a solution to this new problem. They let "Pa" erect two concrete pyramids in the center of downtown business district. One was at Dunklin Brothers intersection and the other was at Redwine Brothers location. Both had signs on all four sides: Drive To The Right.

At first, the horse-drawn drivers thought this applied only to gasoline propelled machines, but several $10 fines convinced all drivers that "Pa" meant everyone when he added to the sign: This Means You.

Two of the worst and most persistent offenders in this day-driving were old Doc Crawford and Loma Jones, the elderly banker. By right of the urgency of his profession, Doc though he always had right-of-way, no matter how he was taking a shortcut. On the other hand, Mr. Jones often had his mind knee-deep in mortgages and foreclosures, and became delightfully vague and absentminded. Both of these questionable drivers had run in's with other drivers and it seemed inevitable that some day they would collide.

One cold blustery morning they finally made it. Both were to blame. Old Doc's sin was corner cutting impatience and the old banker was woolgathering behind the wheel. When both cars stopped quivering, they were tangled up.

Old Doc unloaded, went over to Loma and said, "Holy Cow Jones, couldn't you see me coming around the left hand side of that cement post?" He drew a card from his pocket and scribbled on it "Here's you an appointment for one O'clock. I want to examine your eyes. You need glasses!"

Mr. Jones looked Doc mean in the eye and squalled: "Oh brother, have I got a surprise for you next time you need a loan at my bank?'
– *Mack Stanley*

****

The Wreck That Never Happened In Spiro

Several years ago, two Spiro postal employees (one a part-time farmer) were talking about the right-of-way and priority a mail carrier had while on his or her route delivering mail in town or out in the rural area.

The rural carrier was persistent that his vehicle had the right-of-way in any situation in traffic, stop light stop sign.

The conversation led to who would be in the wrong if a mail carrier with his yellow flashing light ran a red light/stop sign and another vehicle going through the green light/stop sign collided.

One postal worker (the part-time farmer) challenged the rural mail carrier that he would get his old farm tractor and drive it down Main Street and go through the intersection on a green light while the mail carrier would run the red light going down Broadway. They would then collide at the intersection; both knowing what was going to happen.

They would then call the police, have the accident investigated and find out which driver was in the wrong and who get the ticket.

The challenge was never accepted, although the rural carrier still believes a mail carrier has the right-of-way in all traffic situations. The postal worker and part-time farmer still believes his tractor has the right-of-way when the light is green. – *John Clark*

****

Collateral

Our good Indian friend, Charlie Goodnight went into the First National Bank on Main Street to borrow some money. Loma Jones, the banker, knew Charlie from year one and knew his credit rating was good, but like Hiram Nakdimen used to do in the old Farmers Bank, he always had to ask a certain number of questions just to keep it business-like. The old banker new Charlie had a ranch out on Race Track Prairie, so inquiring about collateral, he asked, "How many horses you have, Charlie?"

Charlie Goodnight knew right off. He said, "I got five hundred horses."

Without further questioning Loma Jones made he loan to Charlie. Then a month later, Charlie came in and paid it off. Mr. Jones noticed that Charlie had money sticking out of all his pockets. He said, "Charlie, I'm afraid you'll lose some of that money. Why don't you leave it here in the bank?"

Wiley old Charlie said, "Loma, how many horses you got?"—Bess Stanley

****

Complete Weekend

One day I met Little Bill from Chitln' Switch going into the bus station with a Bible under his arm, I asked him where he was going with a Bible.

"I have been working too hard lately. Sometimes as much as three days a week," said Little Bill, "and I thought I would get away and rest for a while. I'm going over to Hot Springs [Arkansas] for a spell. It's racing time over there, and they say that place is pretty wild when the bangtails are running. Thought I'd just go over and bar-hop my way out to Oaklawn and do a little gambling on some long shots. By the time I get back downtown, the nightspots will be going full blast and I'll do me some dancing and look for some gambling, or something else wicked."

"That sounds enticing," I said, "but why the Bible?"

Little Bill said: 'Well, I thought if I'm still having fun, I might stay over Sunday." – *Mack Stanley*

****

"Groucho" The Banker

Our small home town had two banks, the two bankers were as different as they could be. Since almost everyone in old town had a nickname, the old bankers had theirs. The owner of the Farmer's Bank was known as "Smiley," and the other was called "Groucho," (behind their backs, of course). "Smiley" at the Farmer's Bank went around with an eternal molar-showing grinning smile. It was like he put it on like a mask in the morning. He was a little tighter with his money, but he tried to make the "borrying" as much a pleasure as he could. On the other hand, "Groucho's" rates were always a smidgen less than "Smiley's" but his dour bloodhound look did not make for a pleasant transaction. But old "Groucho" had never turned our folks down.

When Uncle Oscar and Aunt Hannah needed $450.00 to buy a new Ford, they went to "Smiley" first (Hannah didn't talk much, but always went along to co-sign). The friendly owner of the

Farmer's Bank almost met them at the door with welcoming hands outstretched and escorted them to his cubby-hole. Although his smile was just as big as ever, he turned them down for an auto loan. In fact, they had never seen his smile bigger. He seemed to have a gleeful sparkle in his eyes as they looked back through the plate glass door.

"It's never a pleasure to do business with Old Groucho," said Oscar, "but I guess we'll have to get the money from him this time."

They were hardly inside the lobby, when Aunt Hannah whispered, behind her hand, "Oh Lordy Os, I'm afraid you're in big trouble. Look at Groucho."

Uncle Oscar looked toward the banker, and his hopes for a loan fell through his shoe soles. There was a Groucho Oscar had never seen before, he was holding out his hands in a welcoming gesture with the biggest smile you ever saw on his face.

"Huh Oh Hannah," Oscar said, "Smiley's done converted Groucho, and we're out of luck for our new Ford!" – *Mack Stanley*

****

"What we all need around her is a tax BRAKE! "

– *Mack Stanley*

****

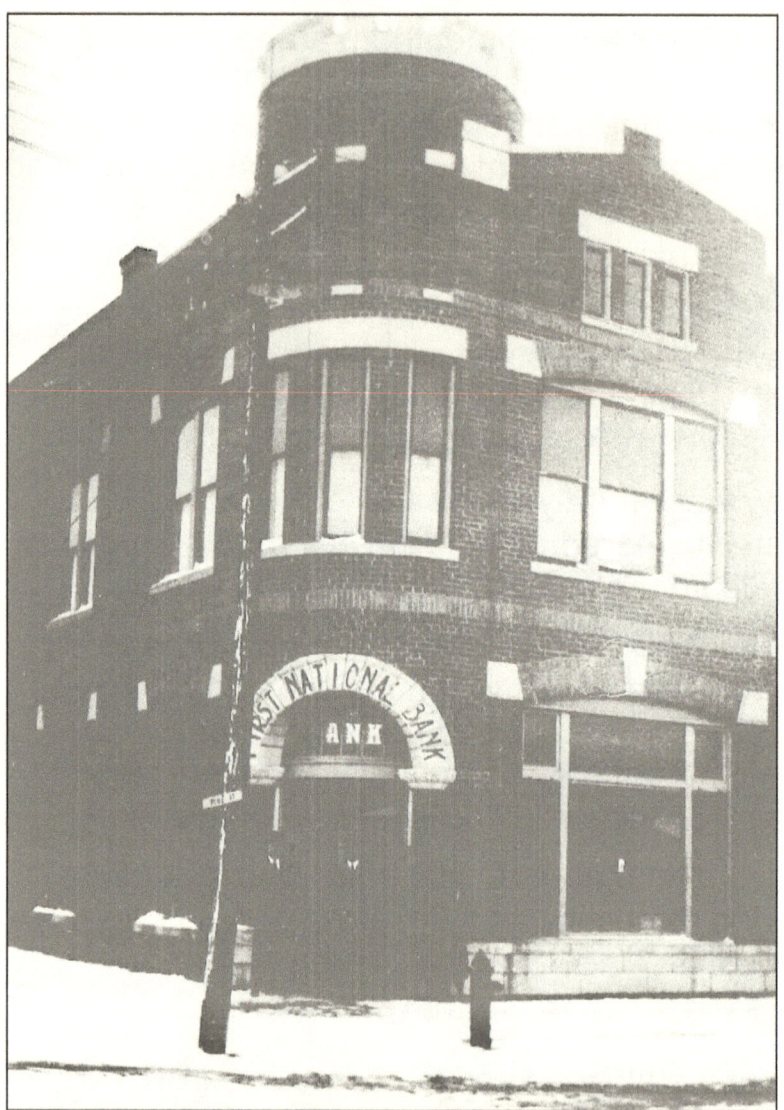

This was the only National Bank ever in Spiro. Some
United States Currency was issued through this money
institution and bore the signature of John Redwine, the
president. Doctor Beckett had his office upstairs in the
back for several years, and some court was held
upstairs, though most court sessions took place
upstairs over what is now Reed's Plumbing and
Appliances. I remember Lant Barran's barbershop next
door, and then a restaurant.

The Walking Banker

In 1922, "Red" Grigsby ran a little chicken and eggs and hides place on Main Street down close to the depot. Red recalls well the first time he saw Old Man Morgan, who later became known as "The Walking Bank," came to town.

Red said, "It was New Year's Day and spitting a little snow, when I saw him get off the Southbound K.C.&S. Flying Crow train. Bypassing the depot, he went straight over to the Port Arthur Hotel cafe and had a bowl of their famous Wild Irish Stew. A few minutes later he came moseying up the sidewalk past my place. He spoke politely. His whole appearance was rundown. He needed a haircut badly. With is coarse gray hair coming down over his collar crumpled straw hat, tattered gray chambray shirt, six-bit denims, old stretchy-sided grandpa type shoes, he was a mess. Under one arm he carried a cardboard suitcase held together by a frayed string of clothesline wrapped around it, He looked like he wouldn't have two dimes to rub together. The reason I recall his hard times appearance so well was that I was flabbergasted that by January 15 he was going around making loans to folks all over, starting that "walking bank" nickname."

That was true. He was soon making more loans than the Farmer's Bank. A lot of folks said it was nicer to get money from him because you didn't have to go though all those ordinary hassles and waiting periods. You paid a little more interest but collateral was easier. He just shelled it out on the street corner in a couple of minutes. Another supposed advantage was he told all borrowers their debt would be cancelled at his death.

We never knew where ol' Man Morgan came from. The old fellow received no mail, and sent none. Not a soul ever came to see him, and he never left town after that New Year's Day in 1922. Many folks worried and wondered about where his lending money came from. I knew the only way it could have come, but never talked about my solution to the puzzle until after he died.

Red Grigsby's curiosity was piqued by the question of where that Old man, arriving on New Years Day in that hard-up garb and the flimsy valise held from disintegrating by a piece of twine, got all that lending money. Red would have been further surprised to learn that when he came to town the handbag did not contain one item of clothing.

It had been completely packed with brand new one hundred dollar bills...– *Mack Stanley*

****

Inflation vs. Good Ole Days

I'm not griping, it only sounds like I am. Right now, my worry of the hour is inflation, sixty minutes from now it will probably be something else. There are certainly enough worries to go around in this day and time. It does look like we would be used inflation after four decades of it without letup. But we just can't forget the good old days. Inflation is where everything is on the up and up, but it is not something that grows on you in an endearing way. It keeps coming on more like a migraine or a chronic bellyache.

The lady of this house and I sometimes wonder if our getting hitched had anything to do with the oncoming of prices ballooning upward. When we stood before Judge Marshal in Las Vegas in 1939 and said the equivalent of our 'I do's', inflation had not yet become a way of life. It was no more than a gleam in the eyes of the money hogs. At that time you could still get a hobble-skirted bottle of Coca Cola for a nickel, a four ounce bar of Three Musketeers for another jitney, that was .20¢ per pound. A good hamburger was a dime, and you could get a bottle of Cooks Beer for another one of the thin ones. You could also go to the movies in Sunny Cal for only two bits, which was already an advance from what we transplanted Okies had paid back home at the Dixie Theater. You could get a steak dinner at the Trona Coffee Shop for .55¢ but back home we could go down to Mrs. Scott's cafe and eat all the chicken dinner you wanted for .35¢

Nowadays, that same steak (well, maybe not from the same cow) will cost you $10.95 at any sit-down eating establishment. And a good hamburger will top a dollar even around the corner at the Eat-A-Bite. Soda pop, even brand X will cost you .50¢ and a 1.5 ounce Pay Day or even a Zagnut will be going at 3 for a dollar 'on sale.' In the very rare occasions when we had to park where they charged back then, it was .25¢ for the first hour and .10¢ an hour after that. The last time I was in the Big Apple, and that'll be the last time forever, the parking rate was $7.00 for the first hour! If I had missed my appointment and been late getting back, the old jalopy wouldn't have been worth retrieving. Then too, an evening out these days may cost you so much you'll have to default on the home mortgage.

It may be well to admit that even in the 'good old days' the wages were not so 'good.' ...
– *Mack Stanley*

****

Gamblers can't trust Town Marshall

When old "Cooncan Dad" came to town he said it was for the purpose of "reading" law at Lawyer Wooley's office. You see, back then you could study law under some supervision of a qualified attorney and finally become a lawyer yourself. But that was not why "Cooncan" came to our town. He came simply for the purpose of fleecing amateur gamblers who thought they knew how to gamble.

No one would let these squatters play in anybody's home, so when the weather permitted, they hunkered down in a little cleared-out place down by the City Lake. This open place made it hard for the law to slip up on them while they were at their sinning.

The town marshal, "Pa" Duncas had been trying to get evidence for months to incarcerate these gambling men. This time he borrowed his son-in-law's hunting coat twice too big for him, put on a floppy old hat, swung a game bag over his shoulder with a rabbit's hindquarter sticking out of the top and cradled his shotgun in the crook of his arm. He put old Blue out in front about 20 feet sniffing and wagging and switching around back and forth, and followed the old hound down toward the half-dozen men hunkered down around an army blanket intensely looking at their hole cards. Little Bill from

Chitlin' Switch called everyone's attention to the approaching figure. Cooncan, whose eyes were no longer 20/20 said in dismissal, "Aw it's just another one of them dumb rabbit hunters."

The old lawman walked right up to the edge of the circle, looked over all the evidence and told them he was going to waltz them right down Main Street all the way to the town calaboose.

"Cooncan Dad" jumped up and down in a tantrum, almost stomping the olive drab bed cover into the ground and squalled loud enough you could hear him upon Standpipe Hill. "That's the dirtiest, sneakiest trick I ever had played on me. If a good tax-paying citizen can't trust his own town Marshal to play fair, who can you trust?"

****

Old Doc Crawford got caught driving under the influence. He had his wife along and you know how bossy she can be in giving instructions.

The town marshal "Pa" Duncas stopped Doc at the stop sign up on the highway. But Doc told "Pa" he couldn't fool with him because he was 30 minutes late for a by-pass operation and his nurse would go ahead and start without him if he didn't get there in time. Then "Pa" gave Doc a four-alarm escort down to the county hospital. – *Mack Stanley*

****

One time during the depression my father offered to give several bushels of corn to a poor family. Although it was a gift, the recipient father asked, 'Is it shelled?' – *Bess Stanley*

****

Bits and Pieces From The Desk of Mack Stanley:

Mack Stanley says his old home town was so small the telephone book didn't have enough people in it to elect a town council.

****

Never take the town drunk home. His wife will accuse you of getting him soused.

****

Jimmy Carter is doing real well. Last year he was farming for peanuts. This year he's building houses for nothing.

****

Note to Mrs. Bill Rutledge:

Yes, Mrs. Rutledge you are right. There was once an open well on Main Sweet in Spiro. This well was on Main Sweet between the Methodist Church and the building we put up in 1945 as Stanley's Cafe and now is Mr. Lawson's Law Office.

****

The Apple Blossom Club

When "Goober" and "Brother" Sullivan opened up their dancehall, they called it the Apple Blossom Club. That was appropriate, as it was built in the middle of their folk's apple orchard. The elder Sullivan's were what we kids called "delightfully vague" and didn't get around much any more. They didn't even know the Apple Blossom Club was out there for the first two years. You had to go up over a knoll of shale and down between rows of apple trees to get to it out in the center of the orchard. Not much to it, just an old barn and a cleared place for a dozen old Fords and such. They always had a good crowd. The weekday music came from a little square Victrola, but the players were the best of the big bands. Saturday nights, we had the "Stoney Point Five" live.

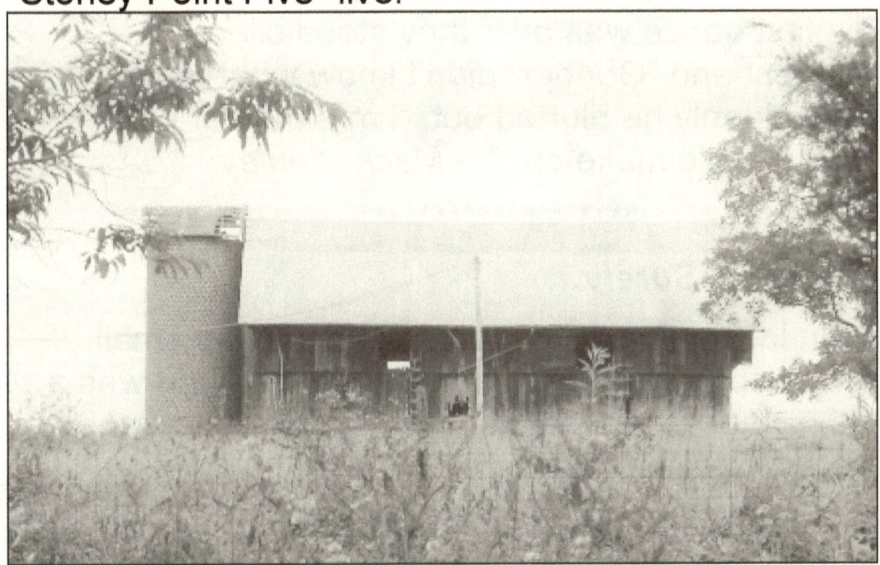

Picture taken in 2009

A few rows over out of sight was a No. 3 washtub full of iced-down home brew sold by "Goober" at .15¢ a bottle. When you snapped open one of those cold ones, blue smoke curled from its long neck and a second made you the best dancer in the bunch.

"Brother" always took the tickets and the door, and was the one who did all the business and talking, and "Goober" was the quiet one who never developed his brother's finesse, especially with the girls. "Goober" was only 17 and given to doing lots of whittling and not much talking. He could go all day on half a dozen words.

When the richest boy in town, sporting his new Jordan Playboy, drove Mary Ann Corden, from the snooty silk-stocking part of town, out to the Apple Blossom Club, young "Goober" must have been smitten with Mary Ann's blonde loveliness. He actually got up enough nerve to ask her for the first dance in his life. All through the first set he did not utter one word. Mary Ann talked all the time. When the first dance was over they stood silent for a moment and "Goober" didn't know what to say.

Suddenly he blurted out, "I'm a man of very few words. Let's make out." – *Mack Stanley*

****

A Rumor, Surely...

In looking back, it seems almost every small town had its own "Hot Tamale Joe." When I was a kid, most of their real names were Jose, and they were of Mexican descent.

Our Tamale Joe was one- legged and small of stature and had a Pancho Villa mustache. He had a two-wheel cart of a box on old bicycle wheels. Big letters of "Hot Tamales" were emblazoned on either side of his box. Hot fried pies were all else that Joe purveyed.

He knew just when to come out in the afternoon and position himself on the corner near the Post Office and holler his wares. There was no free delivery of mail in town then, and going for the mail was more a social function than otherwise. Lots of folks went twice a day whether they got any mail or not.

Joe lifted the insulated top to his box and snapped the heat- sweated lid from on the big lard can, and the delicious aroma that wafted out and enveloped the stream of passersby was unbelievable past words. It seems now those tamales were a foot long mass of succulent meat, chilies and other spices cradled in tasty corn meal and wrapped in a clean real corn shuck. The best part was they were two-for-a-nickel, and his half pound fried pies were a nickel also. Many a Supper had been ruined in advance by this .10 cent feast.

Joe believed he could buy meat cheaper at Scott's Meat Market (where I worked) if he asked for scrap meat for his host of cats. In our small town's constant search for a joke, it was only a jump from "cat meat" to rumors that Joe was making tamales out of cat meat. This rumor being bandied about for only a short while ruined Joe's wonderful tamale business, and soon Joe had to leave town. I never believed that vicious rumor. Nothing made from a cat could ever taste that delicious. – *Mack Stanley*

****

$39.95 Tennises

When I was a kid we were so poor we didn't have two store coupons to rub together. I never thought I'd live to see the day tennis shoes cost $39.95. Back when I wore "tennises" I picked them up for .98¢ at the general store. Even at that price, they were often considered frivolously expensive to some elders. We used to save our shoes for wintertime; they were not to be worn all summer. When we finally used them we always wore out the soles first, and then they looked like a pair of spats flopping around. If we went barefoot too long in the summer knocking around out in Stoney Point, when we put shoes on in the fall, our feet were so rough and tough we wore our brogans out from the inside first.

Of course, today's canvas and rubber footwear is a far cry from those 1920 models, and are of more fancy construction. Their makers would have you believe that a lot of imaginative design and engineering have gone into these modern models. They still look like "tennises" to me.

About all I can say further is that it would have taken a lot of cotton-pickin' cotton picking to get shod in a pair of these up-to- date moccasins, as we picked the fleecy white stuff for $1 per hundred weight American. You would have had to pick more than two thousand pounds of it. Picking up potatoes would have been a more eternal way to buy a pair of footgear at today's prices. Let's see, five cents a bushel is what we kids got for gathering up the spuds in the raw. That would have meant 500 bushels (my arithmetic is loose estimations) and that would have taken about 200,000 stoops.
– *Mack Stanley*

****

The Big Store: Dunklin Bros

When "The Big Store" opened in Spiro shortly after the turn of the century, it was as modem as any store over in Fort Smith. There was even a mezzanine, where the office was located. In case there are a few too young to remember the beautiful mezzanine in the old Goldman Hotel over in Fort Smith that is a shelf-like floor between first and high-ceilinged second floors.

All change making took place up in this office at "The Big Store." A wire track ran from the cashier up there, and out to each clerk's station. A hard leather pouch hung from small two-wheeled apparatus that run back and forth on these wire tracks. The clerk put the sales slip and cash in the pouch and by triggered mechanism, shot it up to the cashier He then shot it back down with the customer's change. There were no cash registers round about the store.

There was no self-service here. A big can-scarred counter was where you shopped with your own individual clerk.

The Big Store had 20 foot ceilings, and to increase shelf space, theirs ran up to the top. A rolling ladder was used that was hooked over a rail at the top with wheels, and had a horizontal track at the bottom which held the ladder out from the shelves and allowed the ladder to be rolled back and forth for the groceries the clerk required. One clerk rolled the ladder 40 feet toward the front, clambered up 16 feet and came back down with a 20¢ can of red salmon. Mother clerk rolled 40 feet toward the back and monkey shined up 12 feet to get a nickel box of Arm & Hammer baking soda. You had to be agile as a mountain goat to clerk in the grocery side of the store. One new clerk took his apron off after half a day. He said he might as well be mountain climbing in the Rockies.

As "Uncle Jim," the senior clerk there aged and became a little arthritic he came to delegate most of the climbing to the junior clerks. He finally got so he kept himself several packages of small items, like Jello and 5¢ cans of Pet milk hid out under the counter. He said, "Skinning 20 feet up and 20 feet back down was just too much climbing for an old duffer like me, just to get a 10¢ box of Post Toasties." – *Mack Stanley*

****

Aunt Hannah Leaves the Dirty Work to Mack

Aunt Hannah was the most forthright person I ever knew, and if you didn't agree with her she could become belligerent. I was afraid of Aunt Hanna is what it was. She failed to show any reticence, and nothing embarrassed her.

She always told it like it was and laid it on the line. One of her boldest and brazen habits was changing the diapers of her current baby on the spot, no matter where the mishap occurred. My aunt always acted like she was in the privacy of her own home, and made the changes while anyone who cared for that sort of thing, looked on.

I was just reaching that certain age when a boy begins to notice girls. It also crossed my mind that it was foolish to live seven miles out in Cache Bottom community when there were so many more pretty girls in Spiro. After reaching this age and that conclusion, I was not long in courting friendship with some of these lovelies by staying with my town cousins as much as I could. I was beginning to believe I was making headway with two nice girls in town. And then Aunt Hannah messed me up!

One Saturday I came through Dunklin Bros.(what we called the big store), and there in the grocery section was Aunt Hannah changing the home-made Pampers on cousin Clemson right up there on the grocery counter. I made a quick turn and tried to ignore her, but she whistled at me and hollered out "Hey Hey Mackie Boy, I got a job for you. Take this didy and poke it down in the wagon bed under the spring seat." Remember I said I was afraid of my aunt. I had seen what happened to others who refused her. I took the diaper and headed for the back door. Forty feet before I reached the exit, I ran smack into the two young ladies I had been hoping to court.

One said: "Hi Mack. What you got there?"

I was struck with dumb speechlessness. I couldn't answer the question. I could only turn red in embarrassment. I darted out the back door and stayed in Cache Bottom for the next three months.
– *Mack Stanley*

****

Cousin Clem Always Prepared For Next Job

Cousin Clemson could never hold a job. After nagging Doc Crawford over at the drug store forever, he finally put him on the fountain. Clem could never learn you had to cleanup as you went along to keep a fountain going. Clem left the fountain area looking like a war zone. After a week, old Doc said, "You're out'a here Clem!"

Clem was a six-footer, no lard, but still a little boy inside. He had a brush of straw hair so spikey straight Vaseline wouldn't make it lay long. One ear was like a little mouse's and the big one on the other side angled differently every day.

Dunklin Brothers gave Clem a job in their grocery department (every boy in town worked at Dunklin

Brothers Big Store at one time or another). Clem was just a passable hand for a month, then he went down to the Eat-A-Bite for lunch and then forgot to go back to work. When it crossed his mind, he was half way through a doubleheader ball game down by the City Lake. He just stayed on to the end. Next morning, Mr. Irby Dunklin, a man of few words said: "You're fired!"

Then, out of the blue, Clemson got a job with Liggett Myers, selling Chesterfield Cigarettes. We all thought the man up above put in a good word for him. Hannah swore it was The Lord. Clemson was furnished one of those nice little Chevrolet sedan delivery vehicles. He drove around from town to town and put up ads and posters and checked stock and passed out a few samples. This seemed a job made to order, but alas, it was not to be. After a month this company served his separation papers.

Clemson said, "I knew from day one them suckers were gonna fire me, but I got even with them before they did."

"What did you do to them" I foolishly asked."

Just to show how Clemson's think tank works, I quote his response: "All that time I was out there selling their Chesterfields, I was smoking Camels."
– *Mack Stanley*

****

Cousin Larnce's Best Friend

Uncle Oscar and Aunt Hannah's three older sons were dating age when baby Larnce came along. These guys loved their baby brother. They fawned over him to the extent that some said, "they carried him around on a stick" meaning they catered to his every whim. One night they found a little black dog and brought it to baby brother.

Larnce and Blackie truly became "A Boy and His Dog." They were inseparable, some said they slept together. Blackie had Larnce's best love and returned it fully. Unfortunately, man's and dog's life span do not correspond in time. When Larnce was 12, Blackie was a very old dog. He was then hard of hearing, his eyes had failed and arthritis racked his body.

The boys came from work to lunch, parked the pickup in the yard and went into the house. Old Blackie crawled under the truck and went to sleep. When the boys came out and started the truck, they were not aware that Blackie was under it. Blackie never heard the motor start and was killed instantly. Sorrow reigned the rest of that day, and Larnce insisted on a proper funeral for Old Blackie. So a proper grave was made beside the barn.

For all that afternoon Larnce stayed beside Blackie's grave in mourning. No one could console him. Oscar watched constantly from in the kitchen. He said Larnce painted something on the side of the barn. When the sun finally went down, Larnce trudged slowly to the house.

Oscar was curious to see what the boy had written on the side of the barn. The father said a thousand words could not have been more fitting. What Larnce had written was: "OLD BLACKIE WAS A GOOD DOG!" – *Mack Stanley*

****

Man's Best Friend

In more recent times, my friend Chooch, in his early 50's coming off a bad marriage adopted himself a dog. Chooch took that dog everywhere; they were so inseparable that Chooch found himself having cross words with the veterinarian when they wanted to keep the dog overnight after a procedure. Chooch yelled "I can't go anywhere without em!"

Many felt that his affection for this dog was unhealthy and that maybe he should seek some sort of help. Chooch told them "I got all the help I need right here" as he patted the dog on the head.

What one must know about Chooch is that by this time in life he received too many citations for driving under the influence, and had to get other folks to do the driving for him from time to time.

It got so that Chooch had to blow into a machine hooked up to the starter on his car, just to start the engine. This would produce a daily breath check on his alcohol level before he could start his car. If it registered too much, his car wouldn't start.

Chooch had places to go and things to do. This was a crimp in his life style. There was no way he was going put up with kind of garb.

Since Chooch spent most of his time in a state of inebriation he often depended on the help of his "best friend" to pass the car breathalyzer for him.

Not sure if the dog got a drivers license, or drove ole Chooch around town, or what happened. But he made it to where he was going. – *John Clark*

****

Where Did Grandpa Keep His Money?

When Grandpa became really old (a little younger than I am now) Mama delegated one of is kids, and that included Little Sister, about a dozen cousins and yours truly, to go downtown with him to be sure he always found his way back home. We all loved this assignment, because being with Gramps was like being with another kid. Besides, grandfather always had money and we enjoyed helping him spend it. Grandpa's money was one of the greatest mysteries in our family. He never seemed to have bills, even one dollar. His money always consisted of silver half-dollars, quarters, dimes and nickels. It was always enough to splurge on whoever had custody of him on at trip.

The older folks seemed concerned about where all this money came from. They couldn't let it lie. They searched and searched, to no avail for Gramp's hiding place for his money. They even checked the bank. He didn't have a dime in there. As for us in the younger generation, we didn't care where it came from as long as it kept coming, and he kept on sharing with us. To stay in our favor all he had to do was keep on buying what our hearts desired and stomachs graved. All our parents sniffed and snooped and turned everything in the house, barn, and outbuildings upside down. They never found the old gent's cache.

For a long time, but not long enough, for us younger ones, we happily escorted Grandfather on trips to Uncle Nat's dark gloomy store for Uncle Sams kisses, fresh roasted peanuts and buttered popcorn, hamburgers at Dad's Cafe, double-dipped ice cream cones at King's Drug and even near-beer at Andy Choates. We would have been welcome anywhere as long as we were with Gramps and he had all that loose change. – *Mack Stanley*

****

Kings Drug Store

Old drug stores were fascinating places. They had something for everyone. For the kids they had the soda fountain with the pull that the young could not resist with its ice cream sodas and sundaes too, with all that expensive toppings like chocolate syrup, crushed pineapple, luscious cherries and strawberries and so on. For Mom there were cosmetics, Dad nearly always headed for the cigar cases first, where at the overhanging gas jet lighter he could fire up something imported from Havana, and grandpa and grandma could replenish their supply of liniment and pills. Kings Drug Store was like that.

This inviting place was where Grandpa and Grandma could replenish their supply of Lydia Pinkham's tonic or Wine of Cardiu and Sloans Liniment and Carter's Little Liver Pills and various other needs for the aged.

Those in their teens and 'Sparking' years could retreat to and make use of the little round marble-topped 'ice cream' tables and sit in the little frail looking wire chairs and let romance take its course.

Those old pharmacies even drew the ladies of the town. Four or more housewives would get together in their early Chevrolets or Model A's and come down for their morning coke. They parked in

front and honked for curb service. This service of
.25¢ worth of nickel fountain cokes entailed as
many as three trips by the soda jerk out there and
back: a trip to get the order, a trip to take it out, and
a trip to reclaim the coke glasses. Nobody seemed
to mind. Our old King's Drug Store was such a
place.

For Mom there was the cosmetics and gift items
and at least the chance to flirt with the idea of
buying the more exotic and expensive perfumes.

For Dad, he always went first to the cigar case
and counter and investigated all the costly cigars,
before invariably choosing a five cent Millionaire
Crook. All those imported ciggaros from Havana
had to be left for other men of more means. Some
of these tobacco sections had an overhanging gas
jet lighter burning all the time for his convenience to
light up.

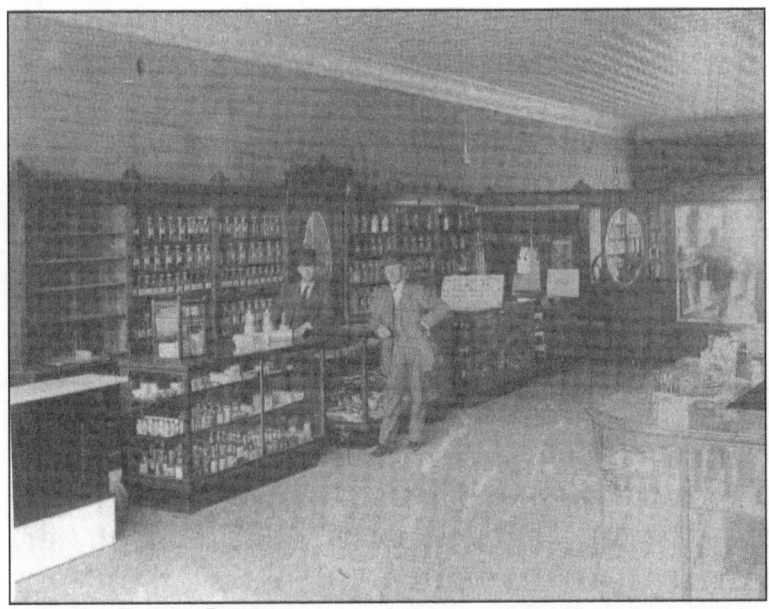

King's Drug Store

King's Drug Store owned and operated by Albert King for 50 years. The Rexall Drug Store owned by Galen Sullins operated in this same building until the 1990's and moved to present day site on Broadway Street.

It is hard to imagine Elbert King as a young man, yet this picture of him behind the showcase proves he was. No one seems to know who the other man was, he was probably some drug drummer.

It is also hard to believe Garvis King worked here for sixty years, as some have said. My remembrance counts back past fifty years. Jim Gilliam also worked in King's Drug Store for many many years. – *Mack Stanley*

****

Good Ole Granny Cheatham

Granny Cheatham is old (Bess says she's older than dirt), this grandmother admits to her advanced years: "I was a good size girl, old enough to spark the boys while they were still digging the Poteau River." She goes on with: Half of me came over on the Mayflower, and they always told me the other half was already here when I came." She could be right, she's half Pollock and half Choctaw Indian. She was probably born about three weeks before the Constitution was ratified. She claims to recall President Washington, says they were kids together, and she used to call him 'Georgie Porgy'. She would have been eligible for Social Security about the time the Titanic went down. She is on her last legs, her first ones wore out about the time Warren Harding invented "Mumblepeg"

On one occasion Granny was angry with the congregation of a certain small church. As she put it, "that little house of worship was just plain too loose." She thought they were not strict or tough enough on the backsliders. On this Sunday morning they were debating on what to do about a young couple's behavior. After much pro and con the preacher announced they would be forgiven.

Granny stood up in the back of the assemblage and indicated she wanted to say a few words. "Brothers and Sister's I've been a member of this church for nigh onto sixty years. And ever since I've been here it's just been drink whiskey and forgive, gamble and forgive, steal and forgive, fool around with the other sex and forgive. It's just been sin and forgive and sin and forgive, and I tell you right now, brothers and sisters. I sure am gettin' tried of doing nothin' but the forgivin." – *Mack Stanley*

****

Preacher May Join the Sinful One

Granny Cheatham was a frail looking little old lady who always wore black dresses and a small gray hat that fit her head like a WWI helmet. She had learned how easy it was to hitchhike all over LeFlore County [Oklahoma] without any cost whatever. It got so that's about all she wanted to do on most days. She would hitchhike 30 miles to attend the funeral of someone she had never heard of until she read the obituaries on the Spiro Times (our local paper).

When you met her on the street it was a miracle if she spoke, even after you had spoken. She did all her talking on Sundays. That was church day. If there was a revival at any of our churches she went day and night. She never had to be encouraged to testify, but she was a downer. She really ran herself down until it was embarrassing to the rest of the congregation. She was sad and longwinded. The gist of her testimony went something like this:

"Folks, I am of the dregs of humanity. I am so rotten that I make all other testifiers sound like angels. I am surprised you let one so unworthy mingle in your midst." She went on and on until she made everyone feel like a dirty dog. She closed with, "I am so sorry that I ought to go in the next room and hide behind the door."

This time, her testimony even struck a nerve with the conscience of Preacher Allstock. He got up slowly, moved to the pulpit uncertainly, and said "Dear Congregation, I don't deserve the Lord's Grace either. I feel like I ought to get back there behind that door with Granny Cheatham!"
– *Mack Stanley*

****

Short Takes by Mack Stanley:

Mack Stanley down at Spiro says he's discovered that old age is middle age with a few more wrinkles, more renounced arthritis and an increasing ability to fall asleep wherever you happen to be.

****

Those Cotton Pickin' Days

We always got up too early when we went to the cotton patch to pick. First, we had to wait for daylight to come to pass. Then, if there was any dew on, we had to wait for the sun to burn the dew off some. The boss-man was no dope, he was too smart to let us pick that damp-heavy cotton that was going to evaporate the excess off before he got it weighed at the gin scales. We always laid to wait for something. Hurry up and wait. I was the junior lightweight picker in the field. Put Uncle Oscar and me together in the same patch and as the saying goes, we could pick more cotton that a gin could gin.

Little Sister was the princess among this field of pickers. Little Miss Priss considered it her special privilege to plop her little heinie down on the tail end of anyone's sack for a free ride. Papa was to blame for that. Little Hazel Willie Marie Tootsie Cusick was a minor goddess in her old man's eyes. Ordinarily, I loved my small sister, but when she plopped herself down on the dragging end of my nine-foot sack, I saw her only as a little fat girl too full of self importance, who added 40 pounds to what was already dragging, and was too heavy to begin with. I felt like a stepson.

I sure was glad when we moved down on Towson Avenue over in Fort Smith, Arkansas. The nearest cotton patch was way over there through Coke Hill in Peno Bottom. – *Mack Stanley*

****

Fort Smith, Arkansas

It was about 1917, we lived where Towson Avenue meets Garrison Avenue over in Fort Smith, Arkansas. That area of town was called "Texas Corner" a lot of folks still called Towson Texas Road then. There stood the Imp Theater, the place I would beg Mama to let me visit when she could spare the .10¢ admission. On July 4th Mama told me "I knew you could find your own way down to Texas Corner and back, I'd let you take Little Sister down there to see a show at the IMP Theater."

Oh, there was no doubt in my mind I could find my way to where Towson joined Garrison Avenue and get my four-year-old sister back to the house safely. I had already snuck out and made this excursion on more than one occasion. After I 'fessed up' to Mama and related a couple of these adventures, pointing out there was no doubt about me bringing Little Sister safely back to her. She seemed impressed, but my mother was a pretty foxy lady for her day and time, although she was only 17 years older than I was. She came up with a foolproof plan.

"You take these two dimes and go down and buy two tickets to the IMP and bring them back to me. That will prove you can make the trip safely both ways, and I can trust you with your sister." She had no sooner finished this when she came up with this: "And another thing, when you cross that first alley back this way from Texas Corner, that runs up behind those smelly old saloons, don't you stop and talk to any old man. One of them will offer you candy to go with him and then do bad things to you."

Those two nickels were burning a hole in my pocket, so I hurried her up with, "Oh, I won't Mama. I'll just skip across there."

And that's how I got to take Little Sister to her first picture show at the IMP Theater.
– Mack Stanley

****

Papa drove a Republic Truck with solid rubber tires for Western Grain Company. He delivered feed, meal and Heliotrope Flour all over town. We lived in a little shot-gun type rent house just south of Yaffee Metal and Junk Company on South 11th Street. On his Saturday afternoons off from work Papa liked to take me down Towson and around on Garrison Avenue. There was a small restaurant in the 200 block on Towson where he stopped and wasted a lot of nickels on coffee. I visited Johnny Massimino in his small shoe shop next door while Papa joshed the waitresses. I liked to watch Johnny fix shoes, he said he would teach me how someday. Johnny was a small man from across the ocean in Italy. His talk didn't quite fit my ears, but I guess I sounded funny to him too. He was not a healthy looking fellow and Papa said it was partly because he went around all the time with those shoes nails in his mouth. Too much iron you know. Johnny and I had a little trouble making each other understand when we talked. We didn't need to talk much though. We had a silent communion. An Okie kid and a man from the Old Country were an unlikely pair, but the twinkle in his eye when he saw me coming, and his gentle smile and pert nod told me that he was my good friend. I was a ten year old Okie kid who would never forget Johnny Massimino.

Papa never took me farther west on Garrison than the Fort Smith & Western depot which was where South 10th now runs from Garrison to Rogers. There was an open front root beer place back east of the depot, and after a stop at the Corner Saloon for Papa, I could easily persuade him to take me there and treat me to a frosty foaming-over mug of this strange nectar. At five cents each, I usually hung around long enough to slop up two or three.

Another character I remember from Fort Smith in the 1920s was Virgil Suggs, the man who was followed everywhere by Ike, his pet Goose. Suggs operated an egg, poultry, and creamery business on Rogers Avenue. Ike was born at Mena, he arrived in Fort Smith as a youngster with 300 other birds that Suggs had purchased for his poultry shop. Ike was originally for sale, but started following Suggs around everywhere he went, became the town pet and strutted anywhere it wanted. He was so smart he crossed city streets only on green lights, I saw that rascal (the goose) for years walking on Garrison Avenue. Suggs would take the goose to Davis Drug in the 700 block of Garrison and feed it Cokes (in paper cups).

When Virgil would go downtown on Garrison Avenue, his fine feathered swan-like friend waddled along behind in his unbalanced, web-footed gait. When he went into a store this not-so-silly goose roosted flat on the sidewalk and waited unruffled for his master to come out and start the goose-step all over. I remember that he was too smart to follow him into a cafe and risk getting her goose cooked.

Ike lived to be 30 and was a fixture in downtown Fort Smith for years. – *Mack Stanley*

****

Overnight Revelation

Uncle Joe Birdsong, down at Alix, Arkansas is the tale spinner in our family. He told us during the depression, as a young man I was tramping around from freight to freight and wound up broke in Fort Smith. I bummed two nickels and bought a quart of milk and a stale loaf of bread and went down by the tracks by a spring to eat and drink. Then a fat girl came up and said, "Where are you going?" I said, "After eating, I'm going over to Van Buren, about five miles."

She said she would walk along with me. Boy was she fat. As we came to Van Buren, it was dark and stormy and started to rain. I said I was going to the police station to sleep. This fat girl said, "Okay, you tell them we're married, and I will sleep there too." So I did.

By the middle of the next morning, I was worried why the jailer had not let me out. He finally came and said, "Mr. Birdsong, I can't let you out. Your wife gave birth to a bouncing baby boy last night." In jail, the men stayed in one cell and women in the other. I guess you must know how surprised I was.

The town people brought clothes and things. One woman brought a nice little basket to carry the baby in. After about 10 days, they let us out, and we started walking out of town. This girl was not as fat as before. There was a hill out of Van Buren and about halfway up I said, "Here, you take the baby in the basket and carry it for awhile. I have to go over the embankment for a minute. Nature is calling me."

I kept the high bank between her and me, and down the branch I went back toward Van Buren. Just as I got down in Van Buren, a freight was leaving, and so was I. – *Mack Stanley*

****

Uncle Web Enjoyed it While it Lasted

Uncle Web grew up on a small farm out between Skullyville and that little round mountain east of Fort Coffee. Until World War One he had never been farther from home than Texas Corner in Fort Smith. When he came home after two years in Europe, his parents were getting old and had let the little place go back to pasture. Webster moved back in with them and although there was no work to do, he stayed on. They furnished food and lodging and Web had a pension of $18 for 'bare essentials', and life went on. After almost 15 years Web received some sort of back pay or bonus from Washington, D.C. The payoff was $1,500.00. That was the most money he had ever seen.

Webster called a taxi company in Fort Smith and told them how to come out to the farm to pick him up. Their first stop was the Spiro State Bank to cash the check. He then instructed the driver to take him to the Goldman Hotel in Fort Smith. There, he was put up in the best accommodations. From then on it was just spending money with Web. Breakfast in bed, napping until noon, and lunch at the Wide Awake Cafe down Garrison Avenue. Afternoons drinking and gambling and goofing off across the bridge in the town of Moffett, what some critics called 'Little Juarez.' Dinners with invited guest in the Goldman Dining Room, parties at the most popular after hours places in town. Day and night, the sky was the limit.

After 14 nights of non-stop fun and games, and spending the money, Web woke up with only seven dollars left to his name. That was exactly the taxi fare back to the small farm in Skullyville. He made the call, and the same driver took him home.

This was neither a funny nor sorrowful Hometown Tale, as Webster put it: "They can't ever take that away from me, for two whole weeks I was a millionaire!" – *Mack Stanley*

****

I Always Thought Poor Folks Was Poor Folks

On a scale of one to ten above the poverty level, I figured there were only two numbers below our family's situation when I was a kid, and you had to go to the Poor Farm way out on Grand Avenue over in Fort Smith to find poorer. A Poor House on Grand Avenue, that sounds like a paradox I think.

We were Poor, that was the most established fact in my young mind. Any hope that this would ever change was neither taught nor preached to me by any of my elders. My first impression was that we were born poor with little expectation of much better to come. Born poor, live poor and die poor. What is to be will be was our dim outlook.

And then something happened, my first addiction became the reading of Horatio Alger's pluck-and luck books. Every week there was a new story of a good boy who won out against all evil forces and bad luck. Rags to riches! That was the strict formula. Each week there was a new name for the boy and a few new twists and situations, but the eternal outcome was SUCCESS!

The Gem Drug Store, on Garrison Avenue in Fort Smith, halfway between the little depot of F.S.&W. railroad and Texas Corner, was my source. These little literary jewels cost .07¢ per copy, and were dispensed early every Thursday morning, and I was usually there before they opened up. I came for my weekly dose of Mr. Alger.

Of course the Alger plot was not very true to life, but after many readings, I gained enough courage to strike out and try, and hope, and even expect. That pig-headness has proven to have been well worth the while. – *Mack Stanley*

****

One of Life's Ways of Growing Up

I don't remember how we wound up in Fort Smith, Arkansas, but that's where our little family was one year. There were only Mama, Little Sister and myself. Mama and Papa were separated then. There was this lady who had a boarding house on Main Street almost up over the theater there. Mama was helping her run it and we lived there. The woman had about 20 regulars there for three meals a day, and usually there were that many drop-ins from downtown. Her dining table was as long as a dray wagon. That dinner was my first encounter with what they called "Ambrosia." That was a mixture of all kinds of fresh fruit with shredded coconut mixed up in a creamy stuff unidentifiable by me. That was the first time we had seen two kinds of meat on the table at the same time, a whole turkey and ham with all the trimmings for each!

I loved Mama with all my young heart and I was completely possessive. When one of the male boarders so much as made eyes at her, I hated him with all my soul.

One memorable afternoon Little Sister and I went downstairs and next door to see the picture show. Then, my worst fears were realized for the first time. Mama was going on a date with a man! My world suddenly fell apart. I was crushed. Why would she want to go and do a thing like that? I couldn't take it, but Sister seemed to be taking it in stride. I never thought anyone could ever come between Mama and me. She tried to console me with grown-up talk, but it was not to be. I followed after them down the stairs and out in the street to the big street car that was to take them on their date. I had no ticket, so I couldn't get aboard, but I ran after the trolley for three blocks. Then, when it got on that big bridge it soon ran away and left me sobbing there. There was nothing left for me to do but trudge my way slowly back to the boarding house.

I grew up a right smart that day. – *Mack Stanley*

****

My First Bicycle Made Me Feel Like I Owned Two Banks

Kids of today on their bicycles amaze me. They perform gymnastics on their two-wheelers that boys of my time wouldn't have thought of trying. Now, in this day and time, these youngsters perform by jumping obstacles, sitting on their handlebars backward, riding over a parking lot reared upon their hind wheels, leaping ditches and curbs and other feats that would cause Evil Knevil to ponder on.

My first bicycle was a $12.00 Excelsior with fancy New Departure brakes and Fisk red-top knobby tires. I bought it from Charlie Winters down on Towson Avenue in Fort Smith. That set of wheels made me feel as rich as Mr. Nakideman, the senior. He owned two banks.

It was impossible for a boy like me to come up with that amount without digging it out two-bits at a time. I would go downtown and hawk the Southwest America up and down the street mornings, and likewise, the Times-Record in the afternoons. Saturdays, I journeyed over the dinky bridge at Coke Hill into Peno Bottoms and picked cotton between my newspaper stints. Another source of income was what I called 'junking'. That was when you carried a 'tow-sack' up and down alleys and gathered anything of value around trash barrels. A good sack like I carried would bring a nickel from my friend Simon Yaffe at Yaffe Metal and Junk Co. When you found a small cache of brass or copper, it was like striking gold! Rare occasions like that made you burst out with: "Happy Days Are Here Again."
– *Mack Stanley*

Mack's Early School Day Crush

When I first went to Belle Grove school down on north Sixth Street in Fort Smith, I was trying my best to get through that stage where I got lockjaw and went cross-eyed every time a girl looked at me. And I was having no success whatever. There must have been something wrong with me besides what ailed me. All a girl had to do was look in my direction for two eye blinks and I turned to stone.

There was this girl named Rozan, actually she had been christened Roseann, but she thought her spelling was more daring and sophisticated. If there was anything Rozan wanted to be, it was sophisticated. She was absolutely the uncontested prettiest girl in the low seventh grade, and she knew it every way a woman can know. One quick look and I thought surely she must be Cleopatra reincarnated. She was 110% aware of what her outrageous flirting was doing to me. Blood rushed to my head and I grabbed for balance in a sea of consternation. And she took fiendish delight in my first dilemma.

Robert Palmer was about the sharpest, most hip, or whatever we called boys like him back then. Already he was delivering prescriptions for Godt Brothers down on Garrison Avenue, and delivered the St. Louis Post Dispatch on Sunday mornings, pulling a little red wagon stacked shoulder high with copies. Robert was well on his road to high finance. He seemed to know all about girls too. I asked him for help, but Robert wasn't much help to me, and besides he was kind of conceited.

He only told me: "There ain't much I can do for you Stanley. You either got it or you ain't."
– *Mack Stanley*

****

The Old Gang

A bunch of us boys (15 year olds) were whooping it up in a little joint known simply as "The Lunch Room." Raymond "Preacher" Priest was holding down the counter. The so-called customers included "Wee John" Brown, "Floppy" Hatter, "Pig" Hogg, "Poorboy" Moneyworth, "Shorty" Angel, the tallest boy in town and me, "Mackson" Stanley.

Then, out of the evening, which was 101 degrees and into the claptrap of six teenage boys feeling their oats without artificial stimulation, strode Harlan "Dusty" Rhodes. "Dusty" was almost 19 and brought the only dose of what we considered sophistication into our midst. He was about four years further down the road to maturity than the rest of us. "Dusty" had already been "away from home" once. He was back on a visit from New Orleans where he had played some football at a school called Loyola, which we had never heard about. He said he had also been a tapdancer (and bouncer) at one of the clubs on Bourbon Street, which was new to us also. "Dusty" said he had ruined one of his knees at football and he didn't have the right kind of feet to last as a tapdancer. His corns and bunions had corns and bunions. He was at what he called "between engagements." All we knew was we would be glad when he left town. Top water minnows like us did not stand a girl-chance with a dude like him around. The most exciting thing we'd ever done was get up at 5 A.M. and deliver the Southwest American out of Fort Smith.

Now, in the lunch room, we all backed against the wall, drew one leg up behind us and stood there like one legged pelicans. Old "Dusty" came on in and sat as near the middle of eight stools as you can get, and called for a Mr. Goodbar. "Preach" served him from the little case with a dime block of ice in the middle and "Dusty" broke the candy bar in half and said, "Half of one of these is enough for anybody." Then he looked around at us with a grin and laid three more nickels on the bar and said, "Give all my friends half a shot of Goodbar."

When we all squatted at the bar, there was only one stool uncovered. Not to worry though. "Dusty" was probably the only 'live one' we'd get that night. - Mack Stanley

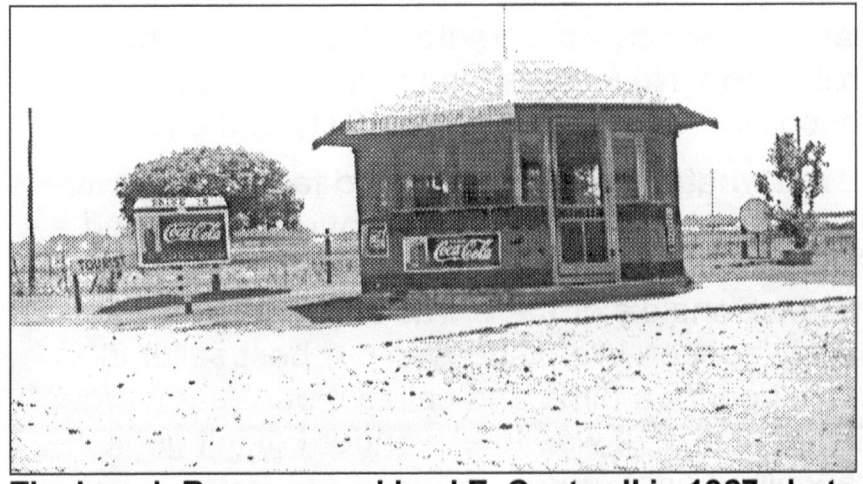

The Lunch Room owned by J.E. Cantwell in 1927 photo. The Spiro school administration building is presently at this site.

Say Mack, Where's the beef?

My introduction to the role of a restaurateur was when I took over the lunch room in Spiro in 1930. The outside physical dimensions of this place were 14 feet wide by 28 long. After partitioning off six feet of the back end for kitchen, the remaining dining area didn't compare favorably with the Goldman Hotel. Our fixtures consisted of six white porcelain stools along the counter and four skimpy booths which held only 16 very serious dieters on the other side. We served what friend Ethan Allen Moore called "a good stew" for 15 cents. Uncle Oscar referred to it as "my Wild Irish Stew." A bowl of 100-proof Oklahoma style chili, bubbling hot enough to scald the hair off your tongue, went for the same price. If your appetite was sorely jaded and you really needed variety, you could persuade the chef to mix those two delicacies in the same bowl. That was what we called a "redtop" because we put the chili on top. No increase in price for this savory concoction. Still 15 cents. Specialty of the house.

But what we were really world famous for (within a 15 mile radius) were our hamburgers. We had a Quarter Pounder long before Mr. Kroc opened his first McDonald's or there was any such known thing as a Whopper. We dispensed our best seller in exchange for a dime and called it our ",Jumburger." Elephant size. It was total wonder I didn't get it franchised right there.

One night, "Squirrel" and "Son Man," two of my contemporaries, came by late.

Now Squirrel had sold shoes down at the 'Big Store' most of his grown-up life. Not exactly a man of letters, but he was always studying a book on the structure of feet. He finally got that all down pretty pat. Whenever you bought a pair of shoes he always gave you a lecture on the Tibia, Astragalus, Calcaneus, Navicular, Internal Cuneiform, First Metatarsal, Philanges, and right on the back to the Achilles Tendon. He never did learn to give you a shoe that fit right, but he sure could talk about feet.

Anyway, I hadn't had a pour all day, but it was evident they'd had too much and were in dire need of some solid nourishment. I made them two Jumburgers, and as they left, they were singing my praises to the tune of Happy Days: "Best darn hamburgers we ever ate."

That weekend, they came by late again. This time, they were sober as two Jude Parkers, but I had been nipping the cooking sherry for the first time. They wanted two more of those good Jumburgers. I made them a pair after some tanglefooted confusion, and as they were leaving this time, their departure was different. Both hollered angrily as they left: "That was the worst darn hamburger I ever ate." – *Mack Stanley*

****

Secret Exposed

Joe Weed and I were about 12 and both lived in that big flat house up on South 14th over in Fort Smith [Arkansas]. One morning we came out with our young bodies draped with enough camping gear to outfit a jungle safari. We trudged down to Texas Corner and waited for a Van Buren streetcar. It came humping down Garrison and clanged to a stop beside the drugstore. When we began to gather up our bedrolls, knapsacks, canteens, pots, pans and enough clothes for around the world plus 50 pounds of groceries, the motorman seemed tempted to move on without us. He looked completely in doubt. He was not ready for us. We hands and kneed it up the steps and sprayed our stuff over four seats, and away we went, swaying and rocking up and down in front.

We had to change cars on Main Street in Van Buren. The first motorman gave us a sickly grin of relief, but the second one was bewildered at the sight of us. This second car took us out to what I recall as "The Smelter," and then we trudged laboriously down a railroad track. It probably was not far, but seemed the longest 10 miles I ever hiked, before we reached Lily Ford, where we camped. We could have thrown a rock to the nearest cantaloupe patch, and we kept a generous supply in the cold water of the stream.

A green cornfield nearby offered plump and juicy ears, and we had "roast'n ears" twice a day until we got old fashioned bellyaches.

On the third day, suddenly a car drove right up to where we were swimming and diving in our birthday suits. Caught "barehanded" with no escape, we tried to carry it off nonchalantly, acting like we didn't mind. A girl, not much older than we were, got out of the car and with no inhibitions whatever, began to snap us with a Kodak. The man, who was much older than the girl, tried to call her back to the car with no success. She said, "That's Doctor Trunkbigger. He's an old fuddy duddy, but if you will come by his office in a few days, he will give you copies of these. I guarantee it!"

When we went to his office, he was nervous enough to thread a sewing machine without stopping it and said excitedly, "Before I give you these pictures, you have to swear to never tell anyone where you got them." He didn't need to worry, we didn't want anyone to see them either!
– *Mack Stanley*

****

Uncle Charlie's Old Black Mule, Tobe

One morning, Uncle Charlie had a little bad luck out near the blacksmith shed. He was trying to shoe his black mule, Old Tobe. The blacker a mule is, the meaner he gets with age, and Old Tobe was coal black and goin' on 19 years old, and was sneaky too. He'll act friendly and pleasant-like all morning for one good chance for a kick or bite at you. Charlie had on his wrong bifocals for shoeing mules and was standing closer than he thought. Tobe saw his chance and took it. Wham! he kicked our uncle six feet high against the side of the barn. That feed house will never stand up plumb again in this lifetime. Charlie just happened to be holding the bridle reins at the time and the kick was so hard it jerked the bridle off Old Tobe.

This mule is notorious for his patience and cunning, but not quite quick-witted enough to realize he was a free mule for a moment. When he did feel free, he kicked up his heels, snorted, switched his tail, and ran for the exit. As he went through the lot gate he looked over his shoulder with a sinister gleam shooting from his good eye and brayed a big hee-haw at Charlie as he vanished.

We're looking for Charlie to come home from the hospital on Good Friday. His trouble was nothing to laugh about but Cousin Larnce tried to make a joke out f it and fell on his face as usual. His attempted quip was: "In view of what happened, it is a wonder Charlie didn't wind up at the veterinarian's."
– *Mack Stanley*

****

Uncle Charlie's Mule Needs a Second Coat of Paint

Uncle always rode his mule when he went to town. He had one little (Kate) that was the sweetest ride you could imagine. Just like sitting in a rocking chair. His other mule (Tobe) was a 'jolter', like riding a wild bull and rougher than a sidewinder. As long as he had both, he rode old Tobe once in a while. His reply, when I asked him was: "I ride old Tobe once in a while just so I will truly appreciate the good ride I get from Kate."

One time Charlie rode Tobe over to Hackett City and tied up in front of the Big Store. While he as inside someone painted Tobe's tail red. Charlie knew all about the beer joint next door, so he figured one of the guzzlers did the paint job. Our Uncle stormed in there like a Panhandle tornado.

All right," he challenged the crowd, "Who's the smart aleck that painted my mule's tail?" The tavern was a quiet as a little mouse for two moments then, the biggest man in the house rocked forward in his cane-bottom chair. It took a whole minute for him to get up to his full height. He was a monster of a man before he got all the way up. He said, "I'm the one that painted your mule."

Uncle Charlie calmed down a right smart. He smiled as gentle as a lamb and said. Well, I just wanted you to know the first coat's dry. Old Tobe's ready for the second coat." – *Mack Stanley*

****

Town Ways The Winner

I always wanted a pony. As a boy, though, I never had one. Heck, I never even had a dog. One Lonesome Luke-looking little hound followed me three miles through a cane break all the way home, but Mom made me take it back right then and there. Two things Mom would never allow around her house were a dog, and catfish ready to fry. If you wanted fish fried, you had to take it somewhere else.

My cotton-picking money was never there in sufficient dollars and cents to buy a pony. I could sweat out only about 200 pounds of the fleecy stuff by quitting time, and at six-bits a hundred, that didn't rack up too fast.

Besides, I liked town ways so well that the next Saturday in town always drained me of any accumulated monetary resources I always splurged for non-essential things like Bevo non-alcoholic beer and Jumburgers, visits to Old Doc Crawford's soda fountain and the Dixie Theater matinee. I also had to buy my own clothes for the coming winter, and the flush cotton-picking season was my only shot. Two pairs of overalls and a gray chambray shirt and a pair of fancy Buster Brown shoes killed more than a month's gain.

Although I never did get a pony as a boy, I later on was able to get some of the trappings that go with a horse. I bought a genuine John B. Stetson hat (about a four galloner) and trod about on Sundays walking pigeon-toed in a pair of Mr. Justin's boots, and traded by overalls for a pair of brass- studded Levis. I may not have had a boss, but I sure looked like a cowboy.

Half a lifetime later, I did win a Palomino Shetland pony at the Spiro Rodeo, and hauled him home in an old high dump truck and slowly dumped him right down into Cousin Larnce's waiting arms. But by that time, I was too arthriticky to mount a regular horse if I'd had one.

I guess I could have done like Uncle Charley over at Poker Bend did. He got so he couldn't get aboard his mule, so he bad his boys dig a ditch they could stand the mule in. Now Charley managed to straddle his mule again, but it's not easy.
– *Mack Stanley*

****

Cutting Wood Without The Noise

When we were kids, Cache Bottom was still covered to a great extent with virgin timber. You could get free wood just by cutting it. Not to say that was an easy job. Most of the wood was cut in cold weather, so we got warmed twice by the same wood. It took only a few minutes with a double-bit axe or pulling an old long cross-cut saw to bring out a good sweat.

Once in a great while we were allowed to take a wagon-load to Spiro and sell it for spending money.

On one of these excursions into town Larnce was lucky. He sold his wood for a dollar. Then a time of relaxation. Larnce always did like to loaf over at Redwine's Store. He could become goggle-eyed looking at all the things that made him dream. That was better to this young fellow than curling up with the Sears & Roebuck's 'wish-book'. That was more like girl stuff.

This time Larnce saw something he'd never noticed before. He asked Mr. Redwine, the hardware man "What's that?"

"That's a chain saw. That is just what you need son. You can cut six times as much wood with it as you can cut with the old axe and saw the way you cut it."

"Could I buy it and pay it out as I sell wood?"

Mr. Redwine said, "Oscar Stanley's son's credit is good here, as long as you pay some down."

My cousin said: "I have a dollar. I could pay .50¢ down." Larnce went home with a new chain-saw.

A few days later he was back in Mr. Redwine's department: "We can't seem to do any good with this chain saw."

The hardware man looked over and gave the rope a hard pull, and the saw burst into action.

Larnce jumped back and shouted: "What's all that noise?" – *Mack Stanley*

****

Uncle Doc down in Greenwood came running into the house and told his wife, "I just came from a rich man's house and he was eating crepe suzette. I've never tasted it. Before I die I'd like to taste crepe suzette."

The conversation continued:

Wife: "I could make some but I have no eggs."

Doc: "Go ahead and make them without eggs.

Wife: "But I have no cream."

Doc: "Make them without cream."

Wife: "But I have no sugar."

Doc: "Make them without sugar."

Wife: "They need brandy."

Doc: "Forget the brandy."

Trying to please, she made crepe suzettes, without all the necessary ingredients.

After several bites, Doc exclaimed "I'll never know what those rich folks see in crepe suzettes."

****

Spiro Fire Department (back then)

Until the nineteen twenties, Spiro's fire department's fire fighting apparatus consisted of a two-wheeler vehicle with wheels higher than your head and a long length of a water hose wrapped around a drum between the wheels, roughly like a spool. This contraption had a long tongue with crossbars and was pulled to the scene by men placing themselves at these crossbars like mules. Eight men could take this big-wheeled vehicle and almost run away with it. After each fire they laid out the hose on a long inclined wooden trestle-like construction to dry. The hoses were cotton and subject to quick rotting if not properly cared for.

Later, when we got our first Ford Model T fire truck, rules about the driver were lax and indefinite. The first driver system was that whichever fireman got there first drove the truck to the fire. Most of the others ran on foot from everywhere and a few came rushing in their own newly acquired autos.

It wasn't long before they had to change that procedure. One time when the fire whistle blew, everyone ran on foot or drove their Lizzies to the fire, thinking someone else was bringing the fire truck.

That was the night the whole fire department stood around and watched Old Man Scott's chicken house burn down. – *Mack Stanley*

****

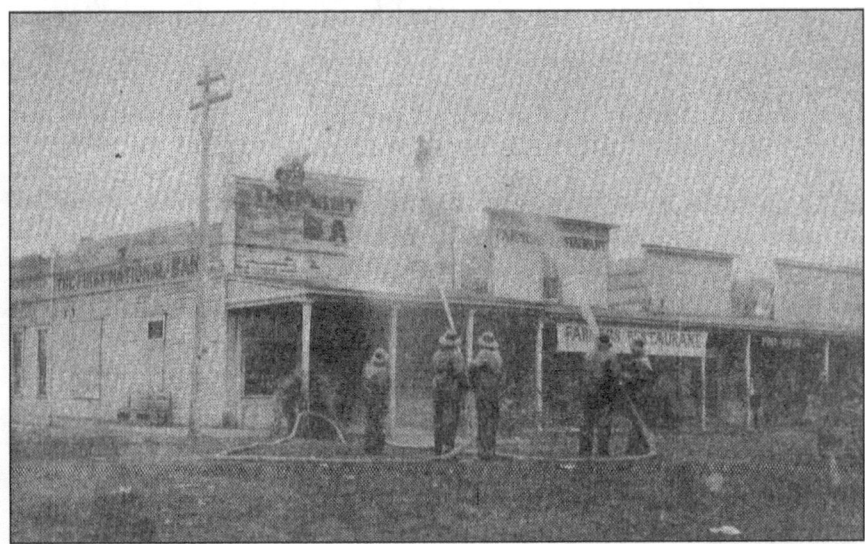

Fire on Main Street

House Fire as a Social Event

Of course, in those so-called "Good Old Days," hometown newspapers didn't have TV schedules printed in them. What we did have each week was a passenger train schedule. It read something like: "Number 4 northbound 3:00 P.M., Northbound Flying Crow 4:15 A.M., Number 6 northbound 10:57 A.M., Southbound Flying Crow 1:40 P.M. Subject to change without notice."

If you couldn't come up with the dollar for next year's subscription to the weekly, the editor would be glad to accept a swap of two laying hens, six dozen fresh eggs, four pounds of fresh country butter, or anything of equal value.

Local society news includes items like: "Sam Scott went over to Fort Smith on business the first of the week." "Miss Wanda Smith came up from Poteau on the Flying Crow and spent the day with her married sister Mrs. Robert Jones." This wasn't outstanding news unless that happened to be your name in the column.

Church news was big then as is now. Some congregations had to share a church building with others. Often, the Prairie Belle Presbyterian held on the first and third Sundays, and Flower Hill Methodists brought the word on the second and fourth Sabbaths of each month.

One day the fire alarm whined in our little town. Telephone Central relayed the information to the editor of the local newspaper. The editor surveyed the newsroom and found no one present except the new young lady whose training had all been as a society writer. Doing the best he could, the editor sent the young woman to cover the fire. Here's the way it was reported:

"A brilliant fire was held yesterday afternoon between the hours of two and four at the residence of Oscar and Hannah Stanley, in the Standpipe Addition of Spiro. A large number of local people attended the function, along with many from out of town. All In all it was an extraordinary event.

Aunt Hannah, as everyone calls Mrs. Stanley, who had just had her hair hennaed, made a charming escape through a downstairs window in her bedroom in an exceedingly attractive yellow puffed-sleeved blouse and miniskirt to match, the patterns of which appeared on our Woman's Page of last Sunday's edition of this newspaper.

The firemen presented an attractive appearance also. All were suitably garbed in like attire of blue, the tunics of which were cut extremely full with the exception of Chief Golightly who is rumored to tip the salon scales at 340 pounds.

The Weather left nothing to be desired. It was quite delightful for an affair of this nature. A strong wind was blowing in a swirling and circulating manner that accentuated the activity for a while. Things were invigoratingly frantic until the wind ceased.

According to one visitor who is present at this sort of gathering frequently, this was on a larger scale than most, with more people in attendance here than any fire in the last several months. It was rumored — and Mr. Oscar and Mrs. Hannah

Stanley have verified this — that the occasion was an expensive affair. The overall cost to them was in the neighborhood of $20,000." – *Mack Stanley*

****

Chief Oscar

At one time, Uncle Oscar was our fire chief. Most of the comment at the time was unfavorable, like: "By the time they get to the fire, it's already out, one way or another."

I recall a fire at one of a nearby city's hotels. The city fire department trucks came, but the flames were roaring so high the firemen couldn't get in close enough to fight it. Then, several trucks from neighboring towns came to help, but had the same failure. Then, with all the bells clanging worse than an old trolley and the old siren barely moaning with a slow, low growl, our town's truck came barreling down the wide avenue, late as usual. All our volunteer firemen were hanging onto ladders and running boards for dear life. The old Model-A rattled into the hotel driveway, threading its way hellbent through the other parked trucks and went right up to the front door and crashed through the plate glass right into the lobby.

Each of our volunteer firemen leaped from the truck, holding a nozzle hooked onto a tank of fire-fighting chemicals, and in five minutes they had the fire out.

The owner of the hotel was so happy about the way they put out the fire, he wrote them a check for $100. He almost went into a rhapsody of praise for our firefighters, "I never saw anything like it in my life. While the others chickened out, you intrepid smoke eaters went right on in to the heart of it." He paused to get his breath. "Tell me, chief, what do you and your fearless men intend to do with the hundred dollars?"

"About the first thing we will do," said Uncle Oscar, "is spend about half of it on getting the brakes fixed on that old truck!" – *Mack Stanley*

****

Crossing Paths with Notorious Outlaw

Back in the early 1930's Charles Avery, (commonly known as Mack Avery) at approximately 8 years of age, dressed in a pair of bib-overalls, bareheaded and barefooted, with my britches' legs rolled up, was wading in a creek call "Holy-Tush", turning over rocks and looking for crawdads. I was about 60 feet upstream from a bridge an old U.S. Highway 271 about 3 1/2 miles southwest of Spiro, when I heard a car coming from the north. It was traveling at a high rate of speed for that day and time, since old 271 had only gravel surface.

When the large sedan approached the bridge the driver got on the brakes and the car slid almost across the bridge. At that instant, the rear door flew open and a man wearing a dress suit (dark-in color with a vest, white shirt, tie, dark had and shiny black shoes) stepped out. As soon as the car door slammed behind him, the car took off spinning it's wheels, headed south.

The man in the suit bailed off the road bank (which at that location was 10 or 15 feet high). It was steep and grown over with brush, but, half-sliding and half-running he made his way to the bottom where there was a three-strand barb wire fence. Grabbing the top of a fencepost he vaulted over the fence and ran under the bridge. He looked around, then he squatted down on one leg to be more comfortable, I assumed, because the bridge was only high enough to stand up under by stooping slightly. That is when he spotted me.

I was about 60 feet from him, standing in the water about half-knee-deep. It seemed to surprise him at first, but then he said, "Hi son!" There was a little silence and then he asked, "Do you know who I am?"

I answered, "No sir, I don't." He smiled slightly and then asked, "Did you ever hear of Pretty Boy Floyd?" I said "Yes," He responded with, "Well, that's who you are talking to. I'm the one they call "Pretty Boy Floyd." By then, I think I replied "Bye", and headed for home in a straight line, which was a mile away.

When I arrived home I tried to tell my mother who I had just seen and she said, "Mack, someone was just trying to scare you, that's all." I could never convince her, but I've always remembered that day, because that was the first man I ever saw in a full dress suit. That image of "Pretty Boy" is still with me as vivid as ever. – *Mack Stanley*

****

Pretty Boy Had Dinner in Spiro

When my wife Bess was a small girl, her mother Huldie worked nights at Clayton's Cafe "up on the highway" as we used to say. After school and other social activities Bess would come to the restaurant and stay with her mother until closing time. There was a shelf under the counter and with quilts and a pillow she had a nice place to snooze when she tuckered out before time to close up.

One night Bess was on the back stool finishing up her homework. Charley Jones, the night town marshal was two stools up from Bess. He had just finished making a round of downtown on foot and was having a cup of coffee.

Brakes squeaked in the half-darkness out front and what looked like an old Hudson touring car with all the side curtains up came to a stop.

The young man who got out and came in through the front door was sort of chunky, but well-built young man with a dark complexion and coal black hair. He perched on the front stool, spoke to everyone and ordered a hamburger, piece of apple pie and drank two cups of coffee, and carried on small talk with Huldie for a while, then became silent. After paying, he said, "Lady, could I trouble you to fill my gas tank?" Huldie went outside and put the gasoline in the vehicle. The young man paid her, and thanked her politely. The old Hudson plowed up some gravel out there in its departure.

Huldie came back inside and as she went around the back end of the counter, she said to the night law: "Did you know that young man?"

Charlie said: "I most certainly did."

Bess piped up with, "Who was that man Mama?"

Huldie said: "That was none other than the notorious Pretty Boy Floyd!" – *Mack Stanley*

Mobile Skating Rink

I remember when a strange fellow came to town in a couple of dilapidated old trucks loaded to the gill with what looked like small platforms. He pulled into that vacant lot on Main Street down south of Redwine Brothers General Merchandise store. He spent a couple of hours unloading, arranging and bolting those sections together, and by the time he went to Busby's Cafe nearby for lunch, there was a new portable skating rink in our town. Admittedly, it was no Madison Square Garden, nor equal to that Walkathon rink in Moffett where Monty Hall got his start as master of ceremonies, but you could actually get up there and skate.

When the rink first came, the best any of us locals could do was get out there and make flailing windmill motions round and round and hope we didn't bust it on the floor. After a couple of nights though, Cousin Larnce was out in the big middle skating backwards. Round and round, pretty as you please and with the greatest of ease. Ever afterward, there was Larnce going round backwards, hour after hour. He's the one who said, "I don't care about where I'm going, I just want to see where I've been." They may as well have made him floor manager, since he was always there.

It was amazing to see how many of us youngsters could put a quarter together so often. I mean two-bits was a lot of money. If we couldn't work and make a few dimes, nothing which could be sold was safe lying around loose. That was more than it took to get into the Dixie Theater and have popcorn, and soda pop. Most of the time, the rink was a better show though. All us kids had expended our cash flow and were treacherously in debt by the time the rink folded up and flew the coop for the next town.

Some wonderful, and a few not so wonderful things happened at that rink: One gal fell in love with the floor manager and carried on scandalously, monopolizing his time supposedly to teach her how to skate. It didn't look like skating to the rest of us. It was a forgone conclusion that she would win all skating contests. Then, when the rink moved on, that girl went with him, never to be seen here again.
– *Mack Stanley*

****

Spiro Telephone Office

Nita Merryman told me she started working for Southwestern Bell Telephone Company in 1919, and worked there for 38 years. Their office was then located upstairs in the Redwine Brothers Store building. The operators on duty at that time took al incoming and outgoing and local calls.

She told me of other she remembered, such as Fannie and Ida Liebe. Molly Malloy, Lula Turman, Jewel Rollans, Bessie Gail Smith, Hula Hiarker, Ozie (Hinton) Harvey, Louis Trolinger, and Cara Schrieber.

The telephone office remained over Redwine's until 1938 when they moved to a new location northwest across the street and stayed there until they went on dial in 1957.

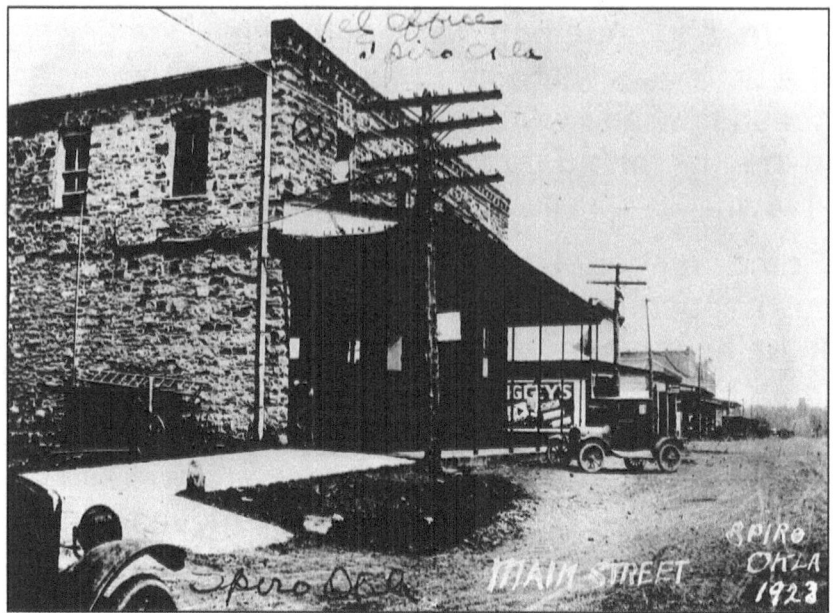

Telephone Office above Redwine's

I remember when a meteor fell here in Spiro. Its force was so powerful it knocked operators away from the switchboard.

Mrs. Odell McMillan told me the first telephone office was in Mrs. Kelley's store building one block east and around the corner to the south from the rest home where Dick Cox had his grocery later for so long. Emma Liebe is recalled as the first operator there and the office was moved to Redwine's about 1908.

There are some old timers who seem to remember that the Liebe sisters may have had a telephone exchange in their home before they moved into Mrs. Kelley's building.

— Mack Stanley

****

Aunt Rodie Got Caught Listening to News

At one time in the long ago, Aunt Rodie (Ronda) wrote the local news for Cache Bottom community for the Spiro Tribune. To point out how long ago that was there has been hardly a house left out there for 40 years now. Rodie, being a nosy person by nature, and newshound by profession, was not above a little eavesdropping on the phone hanging on the wall. As time went by she came to spend a right-smart of time standing up next to Mr. Alexander Graham Bell's invention and listening as quietly as a little old mouse. When our Auntie heard the phone ring three longs and one short, she knew who was being called, but she didn't know just who making the call. That's what got to her! Thus, she did a lot of receiver-lifting as time went on.

What eventually got her caught was her enormous Grandfather clock, which was in this room with the phone. It bonged louder that most and was the only clock in the neighborhood with cuckoo bird that came out and did its act at 15 minute intervals. Every quarter hour the cuckooing came on. That frequency at all hours gave all the ladies of the town opportunity to hear Rodie's clock sound off. For the long-winded one, two or three times.

This became such a common practice, that finally some of the other women snickeringly called out: "Good morning to you too Rodie. How are your today?" But of course, Rodie was way too smart to give any vocal answer.

As time passed, these ladies didn't seem to mind. One was heard to say: "I guess it's worth letting her snoop a little to get our name in the Tribune". – *Mack Stanley*

****

Bits and Pieces From The Desk of Mack Stanley:

Uncle Oscar says he grew up in a small town where everyone dressed casual. He says, "Every time you put on a white shirt, or cleaned the mud off your shoes, some jerk wanted to know where you were going to preach today.

****

Spiro was once so bone dry beer was not allowed inside the city limits. An honest-to-goodness snake bite was the only way to get a shot of whiskey. Uncle Oscar came home one night mad as a wet hen and told Aunt Hannah: "This town needs more than one snake; I stood in line so long today that rattler was too tuckered cit to bite me."

****

Our Uncle Charlie, over at Poker Bend had a bad hangover. After swearing off for the third time this week, he sounded a little like Joseph, the great Indian chief after his last battle. Charlie said: "I will drink no more forever."

****

Another time I ran into Charlie up on Main Street. Boy did he look awful. His hangover was big enough to have one of its own. He was shaking like a Colorado Aspen in a wind storm. He wanted me to drive him out to his bootlegger's place. I was busy and really couldn't spare the time, so I asked him: "How far is it out there?"

"Oh, it's about 8 miles out there," he replied.

He must have seen some reluctance on my face He jumped around like a grasshopper trying to avoid a butterfly net. He became enthusiastic, clapped his hands and chirped up with: "But after I get out there and have a big snort, and then a couple of smaller broken doses, it's only about two miles back." – *Mack Stanley*

****

Soda Jerk

Back in the late 20's, Doc Alston (he was a pharmacist) ran a drug store in Spiro. The other drug store in town had just about crowded Doc out of the fountain business. If you were born less than 50 years ago, you'll never know how big soda fountains were in small towns. They were the main centers of attraction back then.

Doc decided to do something to improve his fizz water business. He would hire himself the best fountain jockey in the country. Doc wrote a letter to who must have been the best in the state. After Doc wrote this whiz, he came down to talk with him. His name was Zeb Block and he was the best banana splitter and soda fizzer in Tulsa. This young celebrity came to town and before anyone knew what was going on, Doc Alston's fountain was number one in our town. Our small city was not quite ready for someone like Zeb Block. He was what we referred to as a 'going Jessie.' We had never seen a young man like this before. Right off, he became the most popular man in town, and Doc's business boomed. Zeb was especially approved and admired by our crop of young ladies, he caused a little fever among certain older married ladies, who should have known much better.

Most of the other young bucks around town tolerated Zeb as long as he didn't try to mess around with their girl. That was hard for him not to do. Flirting and other exchanges were as natural for him as breathing in and out.

Young Block had the constitution of a water buffalo. He was perpetual motion and never seemed to tire. He would work all day and play all night for weeks without rest. He dated every night of the week; soon he had girlfriends in Poteau, Stigler, Sallisaw, and Fort Smith, besides several of our young beauties. Zeb came in from a date at daylight and went right into the store, right on through the day. Most folks in our town were less sophisticated in many ways than this physical dynamo. In looking back, it seems pretty sure that Zeb took stimulants. Most of us locals had never sampled any stimulants other than home brew, a shot of corn liquor, or the tiny lift of a coca cola of that day. Zeb surely needed something more potent, and he worked in the best place for him lobe able to get it at all times.

Common sense would tell anyone that a human body could not go on like Zeb did, but he kept it up for seven years from that day Doc Alston and he made their first deal. I won't disclose just how, but I was the person who overheard those two bargain about the soda jerking job:

Doc said, "I'll give you $5 a day." Zeb thought about that for a moment, then said, "All right, and then I'll take $5 a day." That was the verbal contract that lasted for seven years, but not exactly as both expected. You see, Doc Alston paid Zeb $5 a day, and just as Zeb said, he took another five dollars each day. – *Mack Stanley*

****

A Real Soda "Jerk"

When Cousin Larnce first reached his teens, he began td bug Old Doc Crawford for a job behind the soda fountain in his drug store. Doc already had a good boy and knew what a mess it was sometimes to have to put up with an amateur. He kept trying to discourage Larnce, telling him there was a lot more to running a fountain than double dipping a cone, fizzing a root beer or building a banana split. He tried to point out there was a whole lot of housekeeping you had to do on this job. Doc thought he was getting through, but Larnce hadn't heard a word.

One Saturday, Dick Studebaker, Doc's main man, was unable to come to work, and Doc had to take a chance on Larnce in spite of his wishes. Business was unusually good, and by noon, the old pharmacist noticed Larnce was not making any effort whatever to clean up as he went along. The fountain was already a total mess. Refreshment time seemed to go on at a steady pace all afternoon, and by the time the day was almost over, the whole fountain area was a disaster and in shambles. Chocolate and simple syrup, strawberry preserves and pineapple topping were messed and smeared from one end to the other. Ice cream and milkshakes were spilled all over, and the disaster area was encouraging flies to get killed by the dozens by the slamming door trying to get into the mess. The walkway behind the fountain was a sloppy mess, and wooden floor rack Larnce had been walking on was floating with spilled carbonated and tap water. Soaked napkins, straws, and other spillage was turning into pollution. It was such a mess, a halfway respectable pig would have turned away in disgust. Doc saw that it would take the whole drugstore crew half the night to clean it up.

The old boss man was completely disgusted when he came by near closing time to find a hog pin where there was supposed to be a soda fountain. Larnce failed to understand the old man's painful looks and thoughts, and leaned back against the back bar, propping both elbows up comfortably and lazily said to himself: "There ain't nothin' to this soda jerkin!" – *Mack Stanley*

****

Local Historical Trivia:

A lady asked if we ever heard of a place named 'Hogtown'. I read that Cartersville just northwest of Bokoshe was once called Hogtown. Cartersville's first post office was established about 1891. May have been another Hogtown down around Booneville.

****

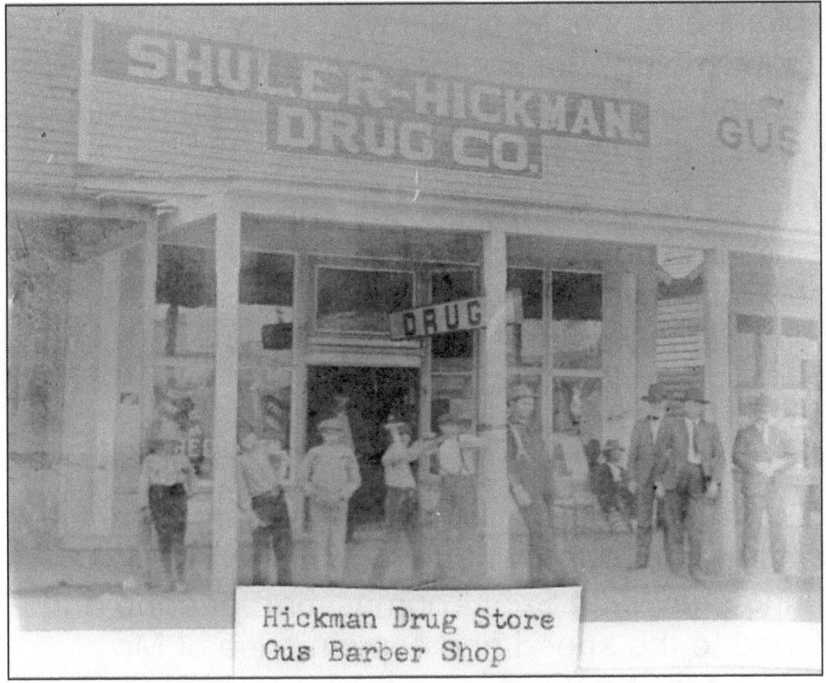

Hickman Drug Store
Gus Barber Shop

Old Doc Crawford's Chicken Scratchin'

Doctors are generally notorious for their poor handwriting, but Old Doc Crawford was an exception. His penmanship was exceptionally sorry.

Aunt 'Rache' (short for Rachel) recalls: "He called it a prescription, to me, it looked more like where an old hen with baby chicks had tried to scratch up a worm in a dusty place in the yard,"

Cousin Clemson had pretty good luck with his last medical formula the old physician wrote for him. He rode the bus to Fort Smith with it. He got in the Joie Theater free. The ticket-taker thought it was a mid-week pass. But they cut him off short at the motel. They told him that was one of the two credit cards they did not accept.

When I took one of my prescriptions to the other drug store in town, the two pharmacists there got in a fist fight over whose time it was to try to decipher Doc's inscribing. Both of them have to get on the phone and ask him for further explanation on his last prescription before they can fill it.

The old medicine man is self-critical about the careless and confusing way he pushes a pen: "I can't read it myself by the time it gets cold."
– *Mack Stanley*

****

The Barber Shop

The End Of An Era: Long after the prominent and leading men of our town gave up getting their morning shaves at Sam Thomas' barber shop and switched to the speed and convenience of Mr. Gillette's new safety razor in their own homes, the old pigeon-holed rack that held dozens, of shaving mugs and soap brushes, testified hauntingly to that long-ago time when important men came to Sam's for that part of their morning toilet.

These magnificent gold layered hand-scrolled and fancifully inscribed cups with the owner's name still on them, seemed to stand at attention in the wooden case, for their next call to duty. That was never to come. It has been many many years since any of these vessels have been used, and the brushes in the cups were mangled loose by inactivity and dehydration and would likely fall apart from the handle if picked up too quickly. There was no reclamation for them. The owners of these ancient accessories were long reluctant to take them home. These antique cups would find no resting place there. There was no need, nor room for them there. So they had been left here together as old friends should be. The pigeonholed rack, the dry hardened soap, the mangy brushes, and several old fashioned straight razors belonging to the most discriminating of the old patrons sat, laid and stood in silent tribute, and proud evidence of that period of time which is now long gone.

After many more years passed, the old mug-filled rack disappeared. No one seemed to know just what happened to it. And by now, not one of those old-timers is still around. But what the heck, isn't that the way of all, flesh? – *Mack Stanley*

****

Our Barbershop Turns Back The Clock

Link Barry was the slowest barber we ever had in our small town (there were two other barbers at the time). Link was so pokey and slow in his tonsorial effort, that almost all his customs fell asleep when he got them trapped in his shop. It would have been better, if the old whacker had been sparkling conversationalist, but his tales were as old as that iron drawbridge between Fort Smith and Van Buren. Sleep inducing, is what his gab was.

One day, John 'Kirk' Kirkpatrick, the butcher on the next corner, barreled into Link's shop and shouted: "That crazy Jumpson Bear just stuck me up and robbed me of $18 dollars!" That was reason to get upset. Then 'Kirk' asked, "Has he been in here today?" No one else got excited. The kooky overgrown boy known as Jumpson Bear held-up someone every month. But he always paid them back when he sobered up.

Link answered 'Kirk's' question with, "Yeah, Jumpson's been in here once today."

'Dad' Gentry had to get in his penny's worth: "Well, that was quite a while ago." Another occupier of the whittling bench took his cue: "Yeah that was a spell ago. Let's see now, Link's cut two heads of hair since then. That was at least four hours ago."
– *Mack Stanley*

****

Nickels Worth More Than Dimes

I suppose you could say I grew up in the 'nickel' days. There are still some around who insist on referring to that period as the 'nickel and dime' days, but quite frankly, I saw forty nickels for every dime that passed my way. In that time gone past forever, you could purchase a quarter-pounder bar of Milky Way, Snickers, or Three Musketeers, or almost any other candy bar for the Big Buffalo Five. A hobble-skirt-shaped bottle of Coke (the real thing) was going for .05¢, and all flavors of Wrigley's product could be had for that nominal sum. A sack of popcorn at the Imp Theater near Texas Corner in Fort Smith, or the Dixie in Spiro for that matter, would come your way just by the passing of the coin equal to five Indian Head coppers. You could even get into the Imp until you were almost six feet tall or had to shave every morning, for a jitney. Then they began to fuss and insisted you come up with a dime or maybe the lady selling tickets could let you owe her a nickel until next time. I think she owned the place.

The local newspapers in Fort Smith were the morning and afternoon newspapers respectively, and sold for a nickel six days a week 'Newsies' like myself had to getup in what seemed like the middle of the night and go up there around Fifth and Rogers in order to keep others from getting ahead and beating us to our customers and thereby reducing our personal grass profit by two cents on every sale we lost. If the press was late getting the newspaper out, you could get awfully sleepy nodding around in there waiting. But you better hadn't doze off, if you did something that foolish, one of the older, and therefore more villainous of the 'Newsies' would wedge a match in between the sole and the upper of your shoe and strike another match to it and you woke in the middle of a frenzied hot-foot dance and didn't slow down until you finished it entirely. Don't forget the skimpy nickel hamburger and ice cream cone that went for the Liberty five cent piece.

But the greatest bargain of all for a nickel was a swaying and rocking ride on one of Fort Smith's street cars. Clang, Clang, Clang, went the trolley. – *Mack Stanley*

****

Little Bill was doing lots of bragging to loafers on the well-whittled bench at the city clerk's office. Larnce pulled a little book out and wrote in it. Bill asked "What's that list of names?" Larnce told him "Guys I can whip." Bill told him "I saw my name, you can't whip me." Larnce looked at Bill and thought for a second, and responded, "OK, I'll just rub your name out." – *Mack Stanley*

Trickery Behind the Ice House

Little Bill from Chitlin' Switch always bragging on himself. One fine sunny morning at the old wooden bench in front of the city clerk's office, he was exaggerating on his powers of memory. He bragged that he could watch a freight train with a hundred-long-string of boxcars go by, and after they had passed, he could call off all the serial numbers on the sides of the boxcars in the correct rotation without getting one of them wrong.

Cousin Larnce became so fed up with Little Bill's boasting he pulled out his billfold and said, "I'll just bet you $10 you can't do that." Cousin Clem held the stakes, and they all moseyed down to the Fort Smith and Western tracks to wait for a freight to come through. (They had to wait so long Clem thought for awhile he'd be late for dinner.)

After a couple of hours, a long freight came through, and as it passed, Bill stood there and read the serial numbers to himself. It seemed to take forever, but when the train had passed and was almost out of sight, Little Bill turned to his sucker and began to reel and rattle off a conglomeration of numbers.

When Bill was out of breath and the train had passed, he turned questioningly and said, "Now do you believe me?" Bill then turned toward Clem, the stakeholder, and said, "They all sounded right to me."

Larnce was dumbfounded. He knew he'd been taken, but since the train was now long gone, he could not refute Bill's claim.

Later, behind the ice house, Little Bill and Cousin Clem split the $10. – *Mack Stanley*

****

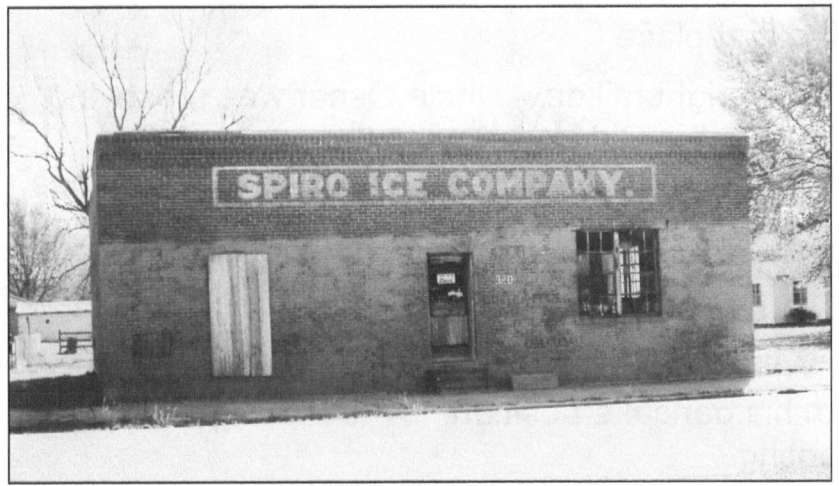

Old ice house located on Main Street (2009).

The old Ice House in Spiro was converted into a print and photo shop about 1975.

Apparently the owner decided enough money was not being "earned" so they decided to "make" their own money. This worked out well until the day when The Secret Service came busting through the door and put an end to their endeavor. It was the talk of the town for several months.

The solid brick building located on South Main Street stands strong today, but remains empty.

– *John Clark*

****

Stately Duty

Anyone who remembers the good old days as such has a poor memory. Everything was not always really good back in the so-called "Good Old Days." Sometimes when two old fellows had a feud on, they stretched it out and made it last long past their remembrance of just what the fight was about in the first place.

One bright fall day, Uncle Oscar was moseying along Nubbin Ridge, enjoying the panorama of autumn, hoping to find a squirrel or two. All at once, he heard a shot, and a bullet whizzed by his bead. Ossie jumped to the ground and made himself as flat as a hog liver.

"What's goin' on over there?" shouted Oscar from his pancake position, "Who's doing all that shooting?"

"It's me, Little Bill from Chitlin Switch," came a bold reply from behind a fencerow of sumac.

"Well, heck fire, Bill, you got awful close to me, you'd best be more careful."

"I shot just exactly where I was aimin'," Little Bill assured my uncle.

Oscar was puzzled. "Why would you want to shoot at me? We ain't got not feud, have we?"

Little Bill said "No, not directly we ain't, but you and Charlie Goodnight had one goin', and old Charlie died yesterday, and left me to take up his side of it. You see, he named me executor of his estate." – *Mack Stanley*

****

Menus From Hard Times

Another dose of hard times: Some of the food we were raised on was later berated about as "poor folks" grub. Little Sister nominated stewed, home-canned tomatoes filled with rarely leftover biscuits as the loser in this category. The bulk of our diet was built around biscuits and cornbread. These were our mainstay. I could take one of Mama's king-size biscuits or a slab of cornbread and build what was a forerunner of the "poor boy" sandwich. And it was a poor boy who ate it. You could take one of those saucer size portions of the staff of life and build a sandwich from anything that didn't bite you first. We could make half a dozen kinds of sandwiches without a slice of meat in the house.

Even catsup (when we had it) or a little mustard in between our bread made it palatable. Cooked dry beans, butter and sorghum, sweet potatoes, anything that filled the in-between. My all-time favorite was Irish spuds fried brown around the edges in a little bacon drippings from a more prosperous past time.

We made many a fine supper on cornbread crumbled in sweet milk (poor boy puddin') and some old folks used buttermilk. We kids would not go that far. White gravy was a never-ending breakfast standby. It was considered impolite to inquire too closely into the origin or ingredients of this pastry batch of the staff of life, because we were all aware that it had been months since hog-killing time, and even cured drippings could not last that long. All I knew was that it was good. An occasional unlucky cottontail, squirrel, or an old hen who had quit laying, and thereby lost her franchise, perked up our menu for a moment, but that was not to be depended upon with any certainty of regularity.

Too much starch or sugar were no boogers to us. It was good that we did not know any better or we may have starved for sure. Cholesterol was not invented then. What saved us, I guess, was the long growing season when we nearly lived out of our gardens.

We were not exactly disciples of Emily Post. We never dwelled too much on what was proper. Uncle Oscar "saucered and blowed" his coffee. Cousin Larnce exercised his enormous "boarding house reach," and most of us were guilty of sopping our bread in the gravy. – *Mack Stanley*

****

Recalling the Oil Boom

I recall "The Last Oil Boom," I was 24 going on 16, and had previously been partners with Will Tharel in a small grocery in Seminole, Ok in the waning days of that boom, so when he wrote me in the fall of 1931, saying he now had a store in Henderson, Texas and needed my help, I went. There certainly was nothing going on at home in the fall of 1931, so I caught the bus to East Texas.

It was a ragtag little line that stopped in small towns at the most vocal and honky-tonkiest eating joints there as stations. We came into the boom area about 30 miles north of Henderson, coming in by way of Gladewater, Kilgore, Overton and Arp. It seemed there were more oil rigs in Kilgore than people.

I saw one place where a merchant had cut off the back end of his store so he could put in one more oil well. After a five year drought before the boom, it had begun to rain after its start and seemed to never let up. Now, the streets were quagmires clogged with abandoned gear from old cars. The scene for those last miles were repetitious, one small muddy one- street hamlet after another. It was like these little cafes had their juke boxes synchronized. For 30 miles it was the same country western balladeer complaining about "Your Cheatin' Heart." I heard it over and over, whether I got off the wayward little bus or not.

About one year before, on Oct. 3, 1930, "Dad" Joiner, with his motley little crew and rusty pipe, hardly a beam and old wood burning boiler, against all saner minds in all the oil companies, brought in The Daisy Bradford No. 3 about seven miles west of Henderson, and all hell broke loose in the biggest oil boom in our United States. The experts had been scrambling ever since, trying to catch up with Dad.

Will Tharel's small grocery was about one mile west of Henderson. As usual, I had to walk the last mile.

There were surely no poorer people than those in this area.

For five years the dry weather had burned them out. For the last year it had rained almost every day. The ones who had some of this poor land went crazy with prosperity when the boom came. One customer at Will's store who had never had a twenty in his jeans before, received enough lease money to buy a new Cadillac and his royalty ran $600 per month, but we had to give him credit for the last ten days of each month. He just ran up and down the road drinking moonshine.

I slept in the store and it was one night there that I discovered a young singer on a 15 minute radio program sponsored by Creamo Cigar Company. He was known then as the "Creamo Singer." He later became better known as Bing Crosby. The talkies were three years old and one night I walked in to Henderson and first saw Boris Karloff as the monster in "Frankenstein." Man, it was a scary walk back down that dark country road after that show.

– *Mack Stanley*

****

Jail-Birds of a Feather

When Cousin Larnce decided for the first time in his life to sow some of the wild oats he'd been accumulating for a long time he disappeared from home for three days. Aunt Hannah was in a stew to know the whereabouts of her youngest son. We had word that Larnce had been seen in Fort Smith [Arkansas]. The informer said he had worked all the downtown taverns, then bought a poke full of hamburgers and a quart bottle of something and checked into the Como Hotel down on Fifth Street. "Oh Lordy Mercy?' was all Aunt Hannah could say at the mention of the hotel. It was time for some action and since I was the one nearest in age bracket, I was designated to track Larnce down and bring him home.

I found he was no longer registered at the Como, so my best choice of action seemed to be to look out all the downtown bars. It proved a hard task to go in and out of all those drinking places and not even have one beer. On my thirteenth entrance I succumbed and had a glass of Lone Star. About every third stop after that I had another "little pour," but being very careful to maintain my soberness. One sinner at a time was enough in the family. I searched all day and until midnight without gain. Then I went to the station to catch a bus home. I still had an hour to wait and the time was already way, way past my bedtime. I was dog tired, so I sat down on a bench in the station beside an elderly lady.

Someone yelling woke me with a start and the little old lady was loudly telling two policemen that I was drunk. "He sat down there and went right to sleep and leaned his head over on my shoulder and I smelled a beer on his breath. I bet he has drunk three or four whole bottles of the stuff!"

Back in those days lawmen arrested you without even reading you your Miranda rights. Those two stalwarts racked me up and soon had me incarcerated in the city jail.

And guess who I finally found...

– *Mack Stanley*

****

America Will Survive

In 1930 I was down in the Rio Grande Valley trying to starve it out through January on an orange grove too young to produce yet. I got a letter from my stepfather instructing me to hurry up to Westville, Oklahoma where he was starting a big job of building a sewer system and disposable plant for them. Since we had been subsisting for two weeks on Musselman's Apple butter and nickel day-old loaves of bread, we thought we'd better check it out.

We (Little Sister, her husband and myself) got in a 1926 Ford Roadmaster with the top missing and went up there to Westville through a couple of snowstorms.

Once there, things looked good at first. Charley put me to work as a form builder for concrete work. We were housed in an almost deserted shack for $10 per month. We survived the first two weeks pretty well and then it warmed up and began to rain. Those first two full 40 hour weeks and wages of .25¢ brought me $10.00. After paying Charley a dollar a day for room and board, I had three dollars left for incidentals. Even in those deflated times that did not allow for many incidentals. The rains came, and stayed, and we loafed. Charley bought a dressed hog from a neighbor and things looked up. Since I was already a butcher I was delegated to dress the porker. I cut it up and laid it on a table on the screened-in porch to freeze the night before we put it away. Next morning we had reason to suppose others were as hungry as we were. Somebody stole our hog meat, except for fatbacks and other skins. And the rains went on...

The third week I got in three days and I came up a dollar short on my board and room. The next week was a rainout. Our provisions ran out and Charley bought a bushel of turnips for .50¢. That week turnips and fried fatback was all that got around to me, unless you count cornbread.

One wore week was all I could take of Westville, Oklahoma. I hitchhiked to Oklahoma City and went up to the home office of my life insurance company where they saved my life by informing me my policy had a cash value of $43.00, although I had been paying $10.40 on it every three months for five years. I took that fortune and went on to California, and things got really tough out there.

Listen up out there! We've been tough times before. Our America will survive this spell!
– *Mack Stanley*

****

Okie From Spiro

When I first went from a little town in Oklahoma (Spiro) to a little town in California in the Mojave Desert, nobody looked me in the eye for the first two weeks I was there. That included my roommate who was from Amsterdam (wherever that was). He talked with an accent that I bet the people in Amsterdam couldn't understand. He was quite a dude and used a lot of toiletries I had never seen before. His talcum had a foreign name, and he kept spraying with something called Jeris. I'll give him that much, he kept himself smelling pretty.

These Desert Rats of Sunny Cal smirked, and accused me of talking funny. They should have been me listening to themselves. I guess it is a good thing I didn't have much talking with my boss or I wouldn't have lasted two weeks. He was from Salt Lake City, Utah and I heard from one of the workers, that he was a full blood Mormon (more foreigners).

After two weeks I was down in the dumps with the Oklahoma Blues and seriously considering lighting a shuck for back where I could call myself "An Okie From Muskogee," and be right enough about that to feel good about it.

There was one guy from Arkansas, but he was a graduate from John Brown University in Siloam Springs. He had a high position in the Lab there and I was only a grease monkey in maintenance. There didn't seem to be much to go for there buddy-wise.

Then I met Melannie, she was a waitress in the coffee shop. I spoke to her and sat in her station, first thing she said was: "What part of Oklahoma are you from? I told her and asked her the same question, and she said "Henryetta." Things took a happier turn after that, and soon the only people who talked funny were Pollocks. – *Mack Stanley*

****

The Best 'Grease Monkey' Job I Ever Had

I had me a good job at the American Potash & Chemical Corporation's plant in the heart of the Mojave Desert. It was just across the Panamint Range from Death Valley, and no less hot. A lot of newcomers here stuck it out until their first pay day, and then were gone with the wind! One hundred and twenty degrees in the shade, with the sand blowing was no place for the weak.

My starting wage was .58¢ an hour, but what the heck, at the coffee shop I could buy their best club steak with a salad and desert for only .58¢. After only eight years I was making $1.38 per hour! About the best job I ever had.

I thought I had found a kindred spirit in a girl name of Melannie from Henryetta, Oklahoma, but she took off with some band leader! She was replaced at the cafe with a girl from Arkansas. An Arkie and Okie should hit it off pretty good in a strange and foreign like this. Well, it was not to be.

Her name was Sally, and she was from Mont Ida, Arkansas. She seemed to get up in the morning for the sole purpose of spending the day honing and sharpening her skill as a would-be stand-up comic. She was a waitress in the coffee shop there, and practiced on her customers. Pretty caustic sometimes! If a patron was slow about ordering, she would bark out: "Elucidate, expeditiously! Did you come to eat, or to ponder? If not to eat, get out yonder," or "Do you need help reading the menu?" If you knew her, you could take her fake sarcasm. Strangers didn't take to her.

When friends came to see me on my job as an oilier in this huge plant, they asked Sally if she knew Mack Stanley.

She quipped: "Oh sure, you mean that 'grease monkey' from Oklahoma who looks like an Arrow Collar ad in his big bib overalls.

– *Mack Stanley*

****

Little Bill from Chitlin' Switch Got Married

We all know that Little Bill from Chitlin' Switch was always as poor as a churchmouse's mouse. But before he got married he went to California and fell in love with a golden girl out there. She was one of the richest girls in Beverly Hills, her father was just about the most important mogul in Hollywood and had millions in the Bank Of America. From the start this great man was against the relationship between his pampered daughter and this young pauper. Besides, he was an Okie.

In spite of this stringent opposition fill and the heiress got hitched. As the young folks were about to depart in Bills 1936 Plymouth coupe, the entire family was gathered around for goodbyes and farewells. The father called Bill to one side for one more attempt to dissuade their folly.

"Young man, do you realize that my daughter drives her own Jaguar, spends more money at ski lodges than you can earn, and can write her own check for thousands of dollars any time she wants?"

"I can't give her all the things you can," Bill said "But we want to go back to Oklahoma and live on what I make. You don't have a thing to worry about Sir." The father was fit to be tied and about to explode.

Bill tried further to placate the older man with: "I love your daughter, I will do my best to take good care of her. You don't need to lose any sleep concerning her." Bill reflected for a moment and continued, "Besides, if things don't work out between us it won't cost you a red cent. Any time she wants to leave me, I'll buy her a ticket all the way home, and I'll personally put her on the bus myself."

– *Mack Stanley*

****

Cousin Clemson's Honeymoon

Cousin Clemson was still just a sprout, but he sure was snappy about Oma Peckingwood. Clem's fatal attraction to Oma came about early on in their torrid romance. He didn't come down to reality until they were married and had no place to live. Oma said they could have moved in with her parents, but they were already moved in with Clem's parents. It just so happened that Uncle Oscar and Aunt Hannah didn't have any of the other kids moved in at instant. The old folks said they could bunk with them until they both got back on their feet.

These adorable kids couldn't afford a long honeymoon, but they did check into the Goldman Hotel in Fort Smith. That was about 15 miles as the crow flies from where they lived. These young folks had a festive dining experience; they dinned in the newly decorated Isaac C. Parker Room. The main course was all the catfish you could eat for .25¢. They had a side order of cornbread, buttermilk and good old turnip greens. For dessert they each had one of those new-fangled Root Beer Floats. That was the first time Oma had ever been out later than milking time. She said she thought they never would get up to their room on the top floor. The Goldman was two stories high, and she had never been higher than a hay loft before that.

They had a glorious time before they went back home. – *Mack Stanley*

****

Uncle Ned Needs a Ride

Old Uncle Ned (no relation) was what we called 'bad to drink'. There seems to be no other way to tell that Uncle Ned was what we called a periodical drinker. He would partake of the wine and other spirits for a period of maybe two weeks and then he would lay off for a couple of days. Ned always thought that each time he had his drinking under control. This time he would handle it, he'd never go too far this time. But Ned could not handle it, this time was just like all the ones before. He always seemed to exceed his capacity and endurance.

If Ned drank more than two weeks, he became too sick to live and apparently too sick to die with any comfort whatever. After Ned reached that stage of two weeks steady 'pouring' the only way he could get back to the world of the sober, was to go down to the county seat and irritate the sheriff's deputies until they threw him in the calaboose for a period of ten days.

One morning Ned came by our house and asked Bess to take him down to the sheriff's office. She agreed, and called out to me where I am working in the garden and asked me to go along. I had on my worst looking old work clothes, floppy shoes and hat and a three days crop of gray beard. But I went along in spite of the way I looked.

It was a short trip to Poteau and a few minutes later we pulled up outside the court house and jail. One of the deputies spied Ned in the front seat and came sauntering out. With no word of greeting to Ned he came to open the door and help him out. The lawman took Ned by the arm and began to turn back toward the jail. Then he saw me in the back seat and spoke to Bess: "Is that another client you have for us there in the back seat?" – *Mack Stanley*

****

Take Chooch to the Capitol

One scaldin' hot July day, Cousin Cotton and his third wife, (he had five) drove up on a one-car accident and recognized one of his school classmates in the vehicle. Ole Chooch was all tangled up in the briar patch and his car was wrapped up in a barb wire fence out on a country road.

This was long before we had cell phones and some folks out in the country didn't even have a land line phone. Somehow the police got called to check out the accident.

Ole' Chooch was known to have taken a drink or two of adult beverages. He was a good ole' boy, but he sometimes did it a little too close to the house.

Chooch was a patriotic Native American, born of proud Indian heritage and one of many that served in the U.S. military in Vietnam.

Police officer Leon really didn't want to fill out a report and mess with all the paperwork. It was just too hot, and Chooch really didn't damage anything or injure anyone, but he couldn't drive.

It was agreed that Cousin Cotton would take Chooch home, rather than the police take him to the county hotel. Back in those days, if you could help a buddy out and the officer didn't want to mess the paperwork and reports, everything was okay. No harm — no foul and nobody got hurt.

Everything was good to go. Chooch was placed in the custody of Cousin Cotton to get him home safely.

While driving down the road to take Chooch home, he insisted on going to the Capitol Lounge, a place where he could continue to par-take in adult beverages. Cotton had agreed to take Chooch home, but Chooch just wasn't ready to go home. He kept tellin' Cotton, 'Take me to the Capitol.'

"Once again, I can't do that Chooch," Cotton said as he drove through town to Chooch's house.

Chooch blew a fuse, he looked up at Cotton's wife and blared out loud — "You are about the ugliest white woman I've ever seen in my life!"

After a scowl from his other half, Cotton took Chooch straight to the Capitol Lounge and dropped him off before he could blare another word.
– *John Clark*

****

Old "Seldom Seen Slim" Can't Stand Kinfolks

Charm can be defined as the quality that visiting relatives have for the first three days of a visit...

Reminds me of when we lived in the Mojave Desert, there was this character known locally as "Seldom Seen Slim." He bore that label simply because he disappeared off up some hot and rocky canyon and didn't come back to town for months, when he had to have another grubstake. When I asked what made him choose to abandon society and take up the hard life of a desert hermit, he made an ugly grimace and gave me the one word answer, "Kinfolks."

Experience with a few of my relatives since then has caused me to realize just how 'ole Slim may have felt. Some of your kin often know just how to make you feel every way but good.

For instance, one of my brothers- in-law, the one we used to see only once a year. Always walked around me looking me over like a head of livestock, and then giving me a grin saying: "Say, you've put on about 20 pounds since I saw you." If that were true all the times he said it, I would now weigh 600 pounds, since I weighed 200 when this clod married my young and impressionable sister 20 years before.

Another female drag is a cousin who never tells me I look bad at the time of the meeting, but time after time keeps saying "My, you look great today. The last time I saw you, you looked like the old devil himself." How can that be when she always says I look good today?

Then there is the macho cousin who invariably gobbles up my $5 steak without a favorable comment, but spends the entire time at the table raving about what a great steak he had over at Uncle Oscar's last night. And Oscar had wine too.

Another is the 70-year-old female cousin who grew up here but moved away years ago. She immediately begins rehashing our childhood quarreling by spouting something like, "Well, here's little old Mackie boy who always had to have everything his way when we were kids or he wouldn't play. He had to be the leader of he'd take his ball and go home. Are you still getting away with that Cuz?"

Aunt Hannah though is one who can make me feel anything but good. After an absence of mine from her, she always comes waddling out to the car and says something like, "Well Good Lord, who'd ever think that a scrawny little three pound blue baby runt like you would ever turn out and grow up to make such a mud fat old man as you are."

After due reflection, I have decided old Seldom Seen Slim was right. Say Slim, do you have room enough out there for one more? – *Mack Stanley*

****

Dad's Boy Helps Mack Build Houses

After our honeymoon in 1939, we lived several months in a two-room shack at the abandoned Stockwell Gold Mine-site in the Mojave Desert. Then we acquired some lots in a place called Argus Town site, one of the countless fizzled-out sites in the desert, where we built a small house of concrete block construction. When that one was finished, we began another nearby. And so on.

Our neighbors on the north were young Larry Brinkman and wife. About all we recall of Larry was that each day after work, he went out in the yard and tinkered with his car for hours. We decided he must have been a frustrated auto mechanic.

On our south side was a couple with an adorable 3-year-old boy named Mike. Little Mike was a confirmed "Daddy's Boy." His father was the center of Mike's life and conversation day in and day out. When his dad was at work Mike took up with Mack. While helping my young husband build houses, Mike was underfoot with endless references to his father. If Mack picked up a saw, Mike said, "My Daddy's got a saw like that." or a hammer, "My Daddy's got a hammer like that." A hundred times ma few hours he informed Mack of this. Even when his father didn't have a certain item, he told that in praise. "My Daddy don't have a wheelbarrow like

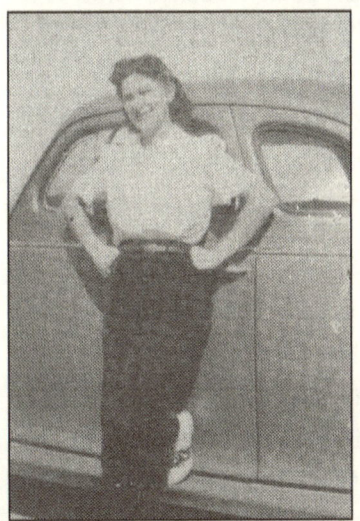

Bess in California

yours, but I bet he can get one.

Both of us adored Mike, but there was a limit to Mack's listening to Mike's father-boasting. I learned when Mack was about to come unwound. That's when I intruded by calling out: "Mike, I think your daddy's home." He left Mack like an old shoe and ran home yelling for his daddy. My calling out was sometimes not true.

On July 4th, 1944, when we left to come back to Spiro, we stopped to see Mike just one more time. Mike was a big boy now, going to school and everything.

As we walked back to the car, Mike's last words were, "My Daddy's gonna bring me to see you sometimes."

As we pulled away, both of us almost began to blubber. – *Mack Stanley*

****

Mack & Bess: A Team After 52 Years

It became evident some decades ago that if the lady of this house and I stood any chance of staying together as a matrimonial team, we must limit certain jobs we did together around the house. Anything requiring mechanical or technical skills we attempt as work partners usually winds up in disagreement that leads to dissension to put it mildly. I say this is the way to do it and Bess says another way is correct. These ventures sometimes end up in a standoff threatening a shootout.

I first noticed this unlikeliness of cooperation in certain jobs together, when we were first married and were building our first little rent house in the abandoned town site of Argus in the Mojave Desert. This project was a little concrete block shotgun type house. Bess had been a very good helper in making the blocks. She put the water and cement in on top of the sand and gravel I had put in the mixer. When we go to the roof she was good at handing the rafters up to me. But when we got to jutting up the sheetrock ceiling, she didn't seem to have the knack. They were only 4X8 foot panels of 3/8 inch sheetrock, and all she had to do was hold them in place while standing under them. After some words, we gave up and I got two neighbor men to help.

One of them implied that I had been too hard on the little woman. I charged that up to youthful thoughtlessness.

It's been like that most of the time since. Even in the house I'm not much help to her. I'm not tall enough to stand flatfooted and replace a light bulb in a ceiling fixture, and too wobbly in my balance to stand on a milk crate. To keep peace in the family, we usually designate this job to the next tall visitor. The only way we can do lawn work is to take separate mowers and each go our own way. Working in the garden at the same time, I do the chopping and Bess goes to another spot and does her thing at something else.

At almost everything else other than working together around the house, we've made a pretty good team for the last 52 years. – *Mack Stanley*

****

Editors Note: Mack & Bess Stanley celebrated their 52nd Wedding Anniversary on Saturday, July 13, 1991. Congratulations Mack & Bess.

****

Uncle Oscar's Bar

When Shorty Perdue decided to go back down to Cajun Country, Uncle Oscar bought his little country tavern over on the state line. Oscar soon became his own best customer. He used to come down before opening and drink his breakfast. As such a dedicated entrepreneur, Ossie needed help and hired his son, Clemson to give him relief with the cash register. Unfortunately for Uncle Oscar, the only thing Cousin Clemson relieved was the cash register. Oscar paid Clemson $3.00 a day to help him, after two weeks, he offered him $5.00 a day to stay away.

My uncle soon gained the reputation of serving the weakest drinks in LeFlore County. When the sheriff's deputies picked up someone was drunk, they took him to Oscar's Bar. After five double shots there, the drinker was sober enough to walk the line. One complainer said it was not so bad to water l00 proof, but beer? The same guy said there was not enough alcohol in one of Ossie's martinis to revive a hung over olive.

Uncle Oscar put one man out of his drinking palace for criticizing the food. This critic said even the doggie bags had indigestion. You may not have liked the atmosphere because of the darkness, but if they ever turned the lights on, you would be very sick.

In the drinking department, Little Bill from Chitlin' Switch was more of a spiller, seemed like he spilled more than others drank. Bill had a unique method of having one for the road. All he has to do is wring out his necktie.

Old Doc Crawford on liquor:

"Despite the great cost of whiskey, a .25¢ drink is still available up in Cookson Hills, a recent autopsy revealed." – *Mack Stanley*

****

An alcoholic is a guy who drinks too much, and you never liked him in the first place.

****

One time Uncle Oscar was so broke he had no Green Stamps.

He wanted to go to Oklahoma City. So he went down to Tenth and Garrison in Fort Smith and caught the Fort Smith and Western Railroad dinky without a ticket.

He hid in the baggage car, but the conductor caught him and kicked him off at Old Skullyville. Then the trainman threw his old suitcase down into the cinders beside him.

From his prone position Oscar shook his first at the departing train and screamed "all right, kick me off if you want." He looked at his busted suitcase and added "but that's no way to treat my little boy Larnce." – *Mack Stanley*

****

Real Estate Business Slow for Cousin Hez in Desert

Back during the Great depression, Cousin Hezzy Tate (I don't talk much about Hezzy) was having a rough time of it. His luck was so bad he couldn't have traded two dimes for a nickel. If he'd had a dollar he would have paid someone to let him work.

An old friend came back here from Darning, New Mexico and said he'd give Hazy a job if he'd work for room and board and commission, Old Ha was desperate, so this guy talked him into going out there to help sell those little two-acre Los Alamos Rancheros. You're seen their signs along the highway. The office of this operation was a one-room shack beside Old Highway 66, and 100 miles from the nearest service station, no matter if you went straight up. This cabin was Hezzy's living quarters. The man said it was easy all Hez had to do was sit in the shack until someone stopped, then take them a few miles back in the desert and show them the lots. He had the contracts and literature and all he had to do was sign them up and get a down payment.

After Hezzy got settled it began to snow. It didn't stop until it was hip deep to a tall Indian and drifting up over the window sills. Hez spent the next 63 days watching the cars go by, eating and sleeping and looking for someone to stop. No one stopped in all that time he had never been so isolated in his life.

Then, on the 64th day, a big Cadillac stopped at the office and a big man fogging a cigar got out and headed for the cabin. Hezzy had not talked to anyone in so long he had become a hermit. He was afraid of anyone and panicked. He ran around behind the office and hid out until the man in the big car left. – *Mack Stanley*

****

Cousin Larnce Visits California

Once when we were back here on a visit from California, Cousin Larnce, who as usual, was at lose ends, said he wanted to go West with us and work at least for the rest of summer vacation. He said if he likes it out there he might just stay and work his way up through American Potash and Chemical Corporation.

At that time Larnce was not exactly odd (that came later) but neither was he your average sixteen year old American boy. He had some health and hygienic habits he was utterly devoted to. On this trip, every time we stopped, even if only for gas, Larnce took his giant tube of Colgate and his brush to the bathroom and scrubbed his teeth vigorously for at least ten minutes. He must have brushed his teeth fifty tithes between Spiro, Oklahoma and Trona, California. He also brought along his own private bottle of Dr. Caldwell's Syrup of Pepsin. He said that was to keep him regular. Can you imagine a sixteen year old boy not being regular in that department?

Every time we stopped to eat he ordered a hot roast been sandwich. Yeah, I know they're good, but for breakfast? Bess said, "With Larnce's countrywide experience in eating this delicacy, he should qualify as a connoisseur of the Great American Hot Roast Beef Sandwich." He wouldn't touch one of these until they brought him a big wedge of dill pickle. He always drank a Dr. Pepper and had a Three Musketeers for dessert.

It was dark when we rolled down into the Searles Dry Lake Basin, where Trona is located. When Larnce got out of the air-conditioned car into the 100 degree heat he almost wilted before he could get into the house. But he didn't say anything and went right to bed.

Next morning we went to work and left Larnce to his own inclinations for the day. After work that evening, we went up to the dining room for dinner. Larnce took a bite of his hot beef sandwich, washed down with a sip of Dr. Pepper and made an announcement that took us by surprise.

"I'm going home tonight. My suitcase is over in the pool hall and I have my ticket for the bus. It leaves at 8 P.M." He seemed to be thinking for a moment, then spoke again. "This is not like I thought it would be. I thought I would see the beautiful Pacific Ocean, live oaks and palm trees waving in the cool breezes and maybe Hollywood. I don't see how you live here. Every day its 120 degrees in the shade and the nearest patch of that is 140 miles to the South in San Bernardino. This sun is hot enough to cook all the grease out you in two weeks."

As Lance departed for the bus, he turned back and said, "At least I learned one thing from this trip. I was happy back home and didn't know it!"
– *Mack Stanley*

****

Timely Exit

Cousin Larnce is sometimes a child of the devil. With a little 'pour' he'd make himself at home anywhere. Maybe even in the Devil's Domination.

On his way back to Oklahoma he was puffing the slots in the Four Queens at Vegas and slopping up those marvelous shrimp cocktails when he struck up an acquaintance with the lady working the next slot. Turned out she was from Wilburton, Oklahoma, fifty miles from Spiro. He asked her if she knew Stoney Hardcastle, and she said yes, he was the best writing teacher they ever had.

Larnce was feeling no pain, and he said to this lady: "I'm going to let you in on a secret. I'm a disciple of that big healing evangelist over at Ada,

Oklahoma and I'm going to show you how to "Preacher" this slot machine." He pulled the handle, slammed both hands open-palmed down on the head part of the slot and hollered: "Heal! Heal!" The fruit wheels rolled round and round and out came a jackpot! By that time everyone was watching Larnce, including the small guy switching around with his little broom on the long flexible handled little pickerupper. He was twitching nervously, flicking cigarette butts carelessly at his little pan and watching Cousin with both eyes. Larnce, who never knows when to quit, told the lady he was going to do it once more so she'd know just how to do it. He pulled the handle again, slapped both hands down on top of the one-armed bandit and hollered "Heal! Heal!" once more. Miracle of miracles! The wheels spun and out rolled another jackpot. Now, everyone in that part of the casino was eagle eyeing Larnce, including some upset-looking Mafia types.

The lady from Wilburton thought Larnce was marvelous: "I've just got to try that now." She pulled the arm and slammed down with both hands and screamed "Heal! Heal" The wheels rolled and out came the third jackpot.

By then, the security guards were inching closer and closer to Larnce and he decided he'd better go over to Diamond Jim's across the street before he wore out his welcome. – *Mack Stanley*

****

Stanley's Cafe

One of our most happy experiences began in 1945. That was the time we built Stanley's Cafe (not to be confused with the 'Lunch Room' that Mr. Jefferson D. Ward, Spiro's first mayor built there about 1924, and Martin, his son operated first).

From the beginning, we offered jobs to Spiro school students and continued to do so throughout the 10 year operation at Main Street and Broadway in Spiro, Oklahoma. The lasting result has been some of our finest memories. During that period we may have employed 30 of 'our Kids'. And anytime we cross the path of any of them today, those recollections are refreshed.

Charles (B.T.) and Roy Dean, brothers in the Wren family, were among the ones who worked the longest. Charles was 12 and Roy Dean must have been around 10. Bennie Cox was another good hand for us, and a pretty bright young chap even then.

Johnnie Davis was another loyal worker and stood up for us against all criticism. His mother worked there also. Mrs. Billi Breedlove was a longstanding good worker for us, and her daughter, Dena Fay, followed in her footsteps and made us a good waitress. Daughters in the Claude Hicks family helped us a lot over several years. Phillip Manke served some time on our corner too. He labored away outside making concrete blocks we used in construction. Mrs. Laughlin worked as second cook to Huldie, Bess' mother, and one morning our dishwasher failed to show and Mrs. Laughlin sent word to her 12-year-old daughter to come and help out. For the next eight hours this youngster got a good breaking-in as a 'Pearl Diver'.

This mother-and-daughter team was here last week for the Alumni Reunion. We couldn't put a name to the daughter but remembered the face well. The mother was 75 and the daughter in her fifties. Another mother daughter duo was Vina and Evalee Jones.

We can be certain we left out many names of equal importance. For that we apologize now.

About 25 years later, after we had retired, Bess answered the doorbell. A robust young man of about 30 something stood there beside a pretty young woman. As Bess opened the door she yelled, "Pinky Dinky!" The young man turned to his bride and said, "There, didn't I tell you that would be the first thing she'd call me?" – *Mack Stanley*

****

While Bess and I ran Stanley's Cafe in Spiro during the 1950's, we put in 12 hour days, seven days a week. When one or the other of us reached near exhaustion, that one got in the car and took a couple of days off. One morning I reached my saturation point and left.

An hour after I left, Bess had a new dishwasher come on duty. This lady was a stranger to us, and because of a small hearing loss, was slightly out of communication with those around her. Real nice girl.

Two days later I came back just before the noon rush. I went right into the kitchen and began putting up orders with renewed vigor and dexterity. The new lady dishwasher didn't know me and seemed slightly awed at the ease and speed I showed at my work. She watched me for a long time. After the lunch run was over, she went up front with a tray of water glasses. Up at the cash register she said to Bess: "Say, that new man you got back there sure is catchin' on fast." – *Mack Stanley* **********************

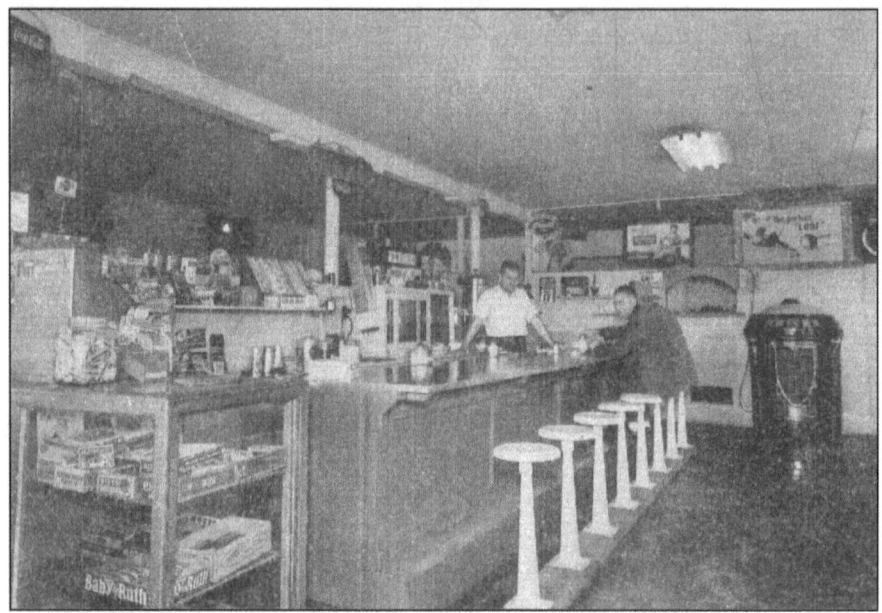

Stanley's Cafe: Yours truly behind the counter

Another time during the cafe period, we came up with a minor identity crisis. Besides Bossy Bessie Stanley, there was two Bessie's working there. Three Bessie's in one small town cafe made for some confusion. Sometimes it was hard to understand just which Bessie you might be referring to.

I think 'Aunt Emma' Lewis, who also worked at the cafe, showed at least a touch of genius when she came up with the simple method which made it perfectly clear just which Bessie you might be talking about. One girl's husband was named John, so she became Bessie John. The other girls' old man was called Mutt, so she became Bessie Mutt. Of course, my Bessie became Bessie Mack in all this change. So everyone finally had it straight and we all, lived happily ever after. – *Mack Stanley*

****

Cousin Larnce is a Slow Learner

Until Cousin Larnce was about 17, the rest of the family suspected that he had only a casual knowledge of the difference between boys and girls. Then he got his first steady job at Ethan Allen Moore's Big Conoco Station, and soon thereafter fell madly in love with the pretty little waitress at Stanley's Cafe across the highway. The main trouble was the pretty little waitress was already married. That may not have occurred to Larnce as a deterrent.

Her husband was a truck driver and always off on his 18- wheeler delivering our Baby Shug brand of canned vegetables anywhere from Boston, Massachusetts, to San Diego, California. Being the young wife of a man who was always on the road again may have been lonely sometimes, so the pretty little waitress may have encouraged Larnce just a little bit. But not to worry. For a change, this time the husband was among the first to know of this budding affair. He went right up to Ethan Allen Moore's filling station and called Cousin Larnce out the back door. For the next 10 minutes, the husband mopped up a 40-foot square of oil-soaked dirt with our cousin. When he was completely finished, he said to Larnce, "Now, every time I come back to town, I'm coming up here and do this all over again. I'm going to keep doing it until you leave the county."

He was away for about a week on his next haul. When he came back to town, he went up and beat up on Larnce once more. The trucker's next load was a short haul. This time, he was back in town in two days. The phone in the station rang, and Larnce answered it. The voice on the other phone said, "Do you know who this is?"

Larnce did know. He croaked a weak "Yes, I know."

"Well," said the husband, "I'm back in town."

Cousin Larnce squeaked a fierce, "Oh, Good Lord, no. This is too soon." – *Mack Stanley*

****

Public Telephones Stink

If there is a harder way to make a living than operating a small-town restaurant, I am happy to say I never bumped into it, accidentally or on purpose. When we ran Stanley's Cafe up on Main Street for 10 years. 12-hour days were less than normal, it was more like 14. If you are going to feed people, you have to be there early and late. If we opened at 5 A.M., there would usually be a couple of early risers already there. Bess often enlisted one of them to help place setups up and down the counter, and another to finish making the first pot of coffee after she started it.

Some of those early-day rowdies thought they should be able to come right in behind you and immediately sit down to ham and eggs and hot java. They wanted to know why you didn't come out an hour earlier so you'd have everything percolating, including hot home made biscuits and a bowl of gravy. A schedule like that and the great need for at least six hours sack-time, left little time for relaxation or entertainment, so we had to create our own as we went along. If we had not learned to laugh at ourselves we'd never lasted the first 10 years. We made up jokes and pranks to lessen the tension and learned to grin and bear it. Many of our customers helped to make the pranks.

About once a week one of them called up and asked: "Is this the little cafe up on the highway?" Going along as the straight man in the routine, "Yes it is," is the way we answered. Then the punch line came, "Well, you better move it back a little, Swink's House movers are coming through town with a wide load." Another one would come on with one as old as the Cookson Hills and wondered out loud if we had Prince Albert in the can. After dutifully answering in the affirmative they'd reply,"Well, my goodness, why don't you let the poor guy out before he smothers!"

Bess' mother Huldie was a wonderful joke teller and not above a prank of her own from time to time. Our telephone in the kitchen was mounted on the wall with the mouthpiece about talking height. That made the top out of sight. One day Huldie put a piece of ripe limburger cheese on top of it out of sight. After a few days we began to notice phone-users cutting their calls short and making faces and shaking their heads. One farmer who used the phone most often, was most effected. He covered his mouth with one hand and breathed in through his nose as if he suspected it was his own breath. He squirmed and fidgeted and looked all around behind himself and twisted his feet around in various contortions, examining the heels and soles of his boots while all us workers were about to explode with laughter. – *Mack Stanley*

****

Blown' Out The Phone Lines

Remember that most offensive old practical joke where grown people who should have known better sent some innocent young boy all over town in search of a 'left handed' monkey wrench. Of course there was no such tool. The way it worked: Some grownup (at least in size) at the blacksmith shop would offer the lad a dime to go up to the Ford Garage and bring back a left-handed wrench they had borrowed. When the young sucker got there and asked for the wrench, they told him they had loaned it to the ice house. They told him at the ice house they had loaned it to the Farmers Bank. It was not there, since they had to lend it to the Owl Cash Grocery. That went on and on until the youngster figured out somebody was playing a trick on him.

Another dirty joke went the rounds until it became known as 'blowing out the telephone lines.' One day someone called Stanley's Cafe and told Bessie the waitress the phone company was ready to blow out the cafe's lines, and if she would put some kind of a bag over the phone, that would keep from blowing dust all over the cashier's section. The noon rush had just begun and Bessie already distressed with hungry, clamoring customers, put a peck (sixteen pound) brown paper bag over the phone, twisting it securely to keep the dust from blowing all over, then she rushed back to the noisy outcry of her clients.

Old Doc Crawford came in for his noon dose of white beans and a wedge of cornbread. He saw the sack creased and crushed around the phone, but was way to smart to ask the obvious question. Cousin Larnce was the first to ask about the phone being in the poke. He accepted Bessie's explanation about blowing out the lines without comment. Larnce was never distressed or curious about anything.

Little Bill was next to question Bessie. When she explained Bill was so insensitive as to laugh out loud in her face, bucking and snorting and slapping his thigh disgustingly. It was at that moment that Bessie realized she had been pranked with trickery. By that time, every customer in the house was aware and laughing and hurrahing Bessie unmercifully.

Then she became plagued (embarrassed) by what she considered harassment. Wilted with self-consciousness she untied her apron and ran out through the back door and did not come back. That served all the guffawing buffoons right that they did not get waited-on and had to go back to work still hungry. – *Mack Stanley*

****

Among Friends

Uncle Oscar lived in Fort Smith [Arkansas] for awhile one time. He spent most of that time on Garrison Avenue. Soon he would call more people by their first names than anyone else in town. His brother Charlie from over in Poker Bend came for a visit, and Oscar showed him the sights. It was astounding to Charlie how Ossie knew everyone they met. They crossed paths with Mr. Nakdimen, the well-known banker, and Ossie went up to him and shook hands and chatted for a moment. Same thing with a couple of other leading citizens. Charlie couldn't believe his brother knew all these important folks. Oscar became a little braggative, and that irked Charlie. "I guess now you'll tell me you know the mayor."

"Sure thing," said Oscar, "I know him well." Charlie didn't believe that, so Os got on the phone and handed it to Charlie, who said, "Who is this?"

"This is Mayor Fagan Bourland, what can I do for you?" Charlie said, "My brother, Oscar Stanley says you know him." "Sure do," was the response, "we have lunch together at the Broadway Grill nearly every day."

The two brothers walked on down the street, and Oscar pointed at a well-dressed man and said, "Here comes John B. Williams, the sheriff, he's one of my buddies." Charlie scooted ahead and said to the man, "Mr. Williams, do you know my brother Oscar?" John B. said, "Of course, of course. Oscar is always helping me out with the kids over at the mule barn. We have a lot of fun taking them all for rides."

Charlie had about had it with Uncle Oscar's famous friends. They walked another block and Oscar heard a band playing, and said, "I forgot to tell you, the president is making a speech over by the post office."

"What? You're not going to say you know Herbert Hoover, I hope," Charlie asked.

Oscar did not reply, but climbed up on the platform and began shaking the great man's hand and chatting. As Charlie stood there with his mouth open, he felt something against his leg. It was a Southwest American "newsie" with a load of papers. When Charlie looked down, the kid said, "Say, Mister. Who's that fat guy up there with Uncle Oscar?" – *Mack Stanley*

****

A Tribute to Marcella Fitzgerald Moore

In all the years that I knew Marcella, she never failed to meet me with a flashing smile of friendship and goodwill. That never faltered or wavered throughout her life. And I am sure there are not many others who did not get this same sunny greeting.

Marcella's father ran a garage in Spiro. Todd Fitzgerald's garage was first located where there is still a concrete floor behind Harper's Insurance. Later he moved to a new building which later housed Amos Caner's county commissioner headquarters, Tibbitt's Market, and still later, Ace Hardware. Marcella was the apple of her father's eye.

Tommy Fitzgerald was her older brother, and there was one older sister. I never knew her mother, but I feel sure she had much to do with developing delightful spirit of this unusual girl. I recall, Todd, her father was pretty stern and businesslike grim, except where his golden girl was concerned.

I can still imagine Marcella going by on her way to school and stopping to give her dad a hug and peck on the cheek. Even that far back, in the last of her little-girl years, Marcella was in love with her school, and it was love that lasted beyond her lifetime, as shown by her great bequeath to the Spiro schools she loved so well.

All through her teens she had the zest and energy of a young colt, bounding and bouncing from place to place, caught up in any school activity. You could always see her pretty blonde head in the center of whatever was going on. Her high spirit and love of life never seemed to lessen with age and in later years Marcella's and Ainsworth's home became the dominant gathering place for those who came to the alumni celebrations. Her home was always open to former students of her alma mater.

Marcella's love for her old school was her magnificent devotion. – *Mack Stanley*

****

Pig On A Bun

Uncle Charlie always did want to have his own business. He said, "I got a great urge to become one of them entrepreneurs." He figured he was on his way when he put in a little barbecue joint out on the big road between Panama and Cameron,

Oklahoma. Although that was sort of an out of the way location, Charlie's fast food eating place was an instant success. Like bats out of the hot place, people were soon coming from everywhere to the "Pig on a Bun". People in Spiro were running over there for lunch, and folks in Panama could be there in three minutes. Over the other way, they came from Pocola, Cameron, and Poteau. Even some of the big county seat lawyers were getting together out there and buddying up like they were all on the same side. Charlie called them his 'regulars'. Stag beer in longnecks was Charlie's best seller.

On Labor Day weekend Charlie had the biggest rush ever. B 11 o'clock Sunday morning he was running out of meat and still the big Monday to come. Uncle Charlie jumped in his old pickup and rushed to Panama. All stores there were closed tighter than a miser's billfold. Ten minutes later Charlie found the same situation in Spiro. He came back through Pocola and Cameron, and the same conditions existed. No meat anywhere.

It was then that Charlie recalled seeing all those loose hogs down in that can brake in the Poker Bend of the Poteau River. "I golly," he said to himself," I got to have meat, I know these hogs belong to someone, but maybe I can pay them later," It was not a hard task talking himself into killing someone else's porker. He found a nice white hog that would dress out about 230 pounds, shot it, and loaded it in the bed of his pickup, covered it with an old quilt and headed back toward the "Pig-on-a-Bun."

Charlie was in a hurry, so he speeded up a bit, while there were no Highway Patrol back in there, it was Charlie's bad luck to run onto a county deputy sheriff poking around. Our uncle's haste caused the deputy to chase after and pull him over.

"I golly Charlie. What's up? I never saw you do more 'n 30 in my whole life."

"Oh howdy Windy. It's my brother Doc from over at Greenwood Arkansas. He's sick back there in my pickup bed. He cut himself bad with one of them new chain saws."

Windy leaned over the tailgate and raised the edge of the old quit for a short look. "Well," he said, "I'm gonna let you go this time Charlie, but be careful down in here. And by the way, tell your "brother," I said he was the ugliest man in LeFlore county."

– Mack Stanley

****

Cousin Larnce Got Caught Left Handed

In his hunting expeditions, young Cousin Larnce explored the entire county. Once in a while he would get lost but unfortunately never permanently. He seemed to have a homing instinct equal to that of a pigeon.

One time he stopped at a hillbilly's shack for a drink of water. An old man was sprawled out on the front porch in a hammock taking his eternal ease.

When Larnce approached the man he asked "Can I get a drink?"

"Shore, hep yourself. There's the bucket on the bench across the end of the porch there." By now Larnce was close enough for a good look at the old hillbilly. Larnce thought he was the dirtiest, nastiest looking human he had ever encountered. He looked like his nastiness had been soaked and ground in. His bearded face was a tangled mess, and his hands and bare feet were potty also.

Larnce approached the water bucket and gourd dipper with hesitation. He looked back at the old man lying in his own filth and lost his thirst completely. Then the man turned over on his side, Larnce knew he couldn't stop now, he had to take a drink or risk the hillbilly's ire. Larnce thought he knew how to lessen the ordeal of having to drink from the gourd. He picked up the gourd with his left hand and drank from it in that awkward position. The old dirty man still lay on his side with his head resting in one of his hands. He slapped his dusty overalled thigh, split the tangled mass around his mouth with a nasty grin and said, "I golly Boy, You're the onliest one who drinks out of a gourd dipper just like I do, with my left hand."
– *Mack Stanley*

****

Take the Berdoo

In search of work Cousin Larnce left home and hitchhiked to sunny California. He got a job and saved a few bucks. Everything was ok except Larnce had no social life. He knew no women out there in California and didn't know how to meet new ones. One of his coworkers knew of his dilemma and offered some advice. "No problem," said the friend, "here's what you do. Take off early this afternoon and catch the Big Red car marked Berdoo. That is short for San Bernardino. Ride it out to Ontario and get off. There will be a bunch of good-looking women waiting there for their commuting husbands in their station wagons. There's bound to be one whose husband missed the trolley. She will be disappointed and lonely, and you can strike up an acquaintance with her."

That afternoon Larnce took his co-worker's advice and caught the Berdoo car. But Larnce dozed off and went past the intended destination. Oh well, he thought, another town will be all right, and so he got off at the next town. It was just like the man had said it would be in Ontario. Half a dozen attractive women were sitting in their cars. One was disappointed because her husband had not caught the car. Larnce saw she looked sort of forlorn and lonely, so he went over and offered conversation to her. She was in a receptive mood and invited Larnce home with her for a drink.

Less than an hour later the husband stormed in, and blew his stack at his wife in a furious manner.

After a loud bawling out to the woman, the man turned to Larnce and shouted even louder, "And as for you. I told you to get off at Ontario."
– *Mack Stanley*

****

New Doctor in Spiro

Old Doc Crawford was the only doctor in town from Indian Territory days until almost the twenties. Then a young dude from Fort Smith named Dr.

W.B. Gibb moved in and set up practice. Old Doc had treated most all of us all our lives and brought nearly all of us under 50 into this world, or helped, as he put it. Any new doctor coming into Spiro, Oklahoma to horn in on his practice would have a few pills to swallow himself.

The first 30 days nobody saw much of the new physician. He just sat up there in his lonely little office over the bank and waited for patients who didn't come in droves. Then all of a sudden, things seemed to pick up. Young Doc would come trotting down the iron stairs outside the bank, jump into his new Star and take off ahead of a cloud of dust across the F.S. & W. tracks toward Fairview community. Then an hour later he would come back into town from another direction. An hour later, he would come scrambling back down to his car and jump through all that action again. All this activity began to attract the attention of the town folks. Some thought if he was getting all that much business out in the country he must be pretty good, so town folks began to visit Young Doc, and word spread that he was a good doctor.

Uncle Oscar was one of the diehard skeptics concerning anything new. He was also as suspicious and nosey as a town dog. One day when Young Doc took off frantically for the country, Ossie followed in his Willis-Knight touring car. He said the young physician drove like a bat out of the hot placed until he came to Good Water Creek, then parked under a tree for an hour's snooze. Later, he drove around two sections and came back in from the northwest without stopping again. Uncle Oscar confirmed his worst suspicions. Young Doc was trying to make town folks think he had lots of patients out in the country, and by now it was working. Then, as soon as the farm people saw townies going to Young Doc, they began to do like wise.

What did Old Doc Crawford think of this dubious competition? Most older would have resented the young squirt, but not Old Doc. In answer to this question, the elder physician looked far off, and for one the very few times, talked over most of our heads. He said: "I like that boy. He's assiduously industrious!" – *Mack Stanley*

****

Pictured Right is an early picture of the Choctaw Commercial Bank on Main Street Spiro. You might consider it the forerunner or ancestor of the present Spiro State Bank. At the time of this photograph, this was the only brick building in Spiro, Indian Territory. At first several fraternal lodges were headquartered upstairs. Later, Doctor Gilliam (among others) had his office up there for several years, as well as various lawyers, including E.T. Watkins. This bank was a state and county depository, and had the grand Capital and Surplus of $23,000.00 which was four times what some of the smaller banks had in that day. If memory serves, The First National Bank in Fort Smith, had started several years before that with less.
This building is now the home of John Clark's fine weekly newspaper, the Spiro Graphic.

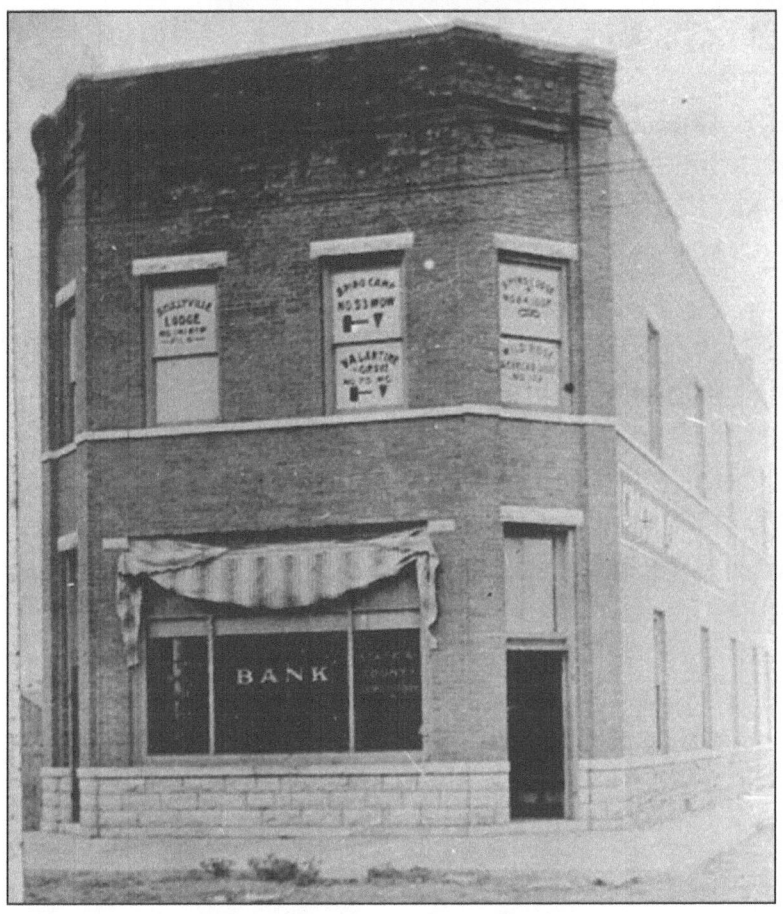

Small Town Doctors

Back in the early days of the approach to my teens, small-town doctors were rated right tip there next to Jesus by a lot of us common folk. A doctor may as well not had a first name then. After he hung out his M.D. shingle he became Doctor Gilham, Doctor Mixon, Doctor Beckett or Doctor Moody, the last being the only black M.D. we ever had in our midst. These were the best remembered by me. Even the wives of these great men often referred to their husbands names in hushed reverence. Never a pet or nickname, nor anything as personal as a first name. I never knew the first name of most of them. The nearest I ever came was Doctor A.M. Mixon. His oldest son was named Aaron Malachi. We kids referred to our friend as Big A little a r-o-n. Aaron was probably the doctor's name also.

As the delivery boy at Scott's Meat Market I had occasion to hear a lot of doctor's wives speak of their spouses. In their kitchens, they might refer to them simply as 'doctor', but you knew that if she had been writing, she wood have spelled it DOCTOR in capital letters. Not even abbreviated to DR. They said things like: "Wait while I check these steaks, DOCTOR will only eat the five choice T-bones in a hindquarter, and those only from the tight kidney side. Doctor is pretty finicky, you know." After these inspections, she either rejected them or mumbled grudgingly, "I guess maybe they'll do." Never any enthusiasm, even if they were prime.

All four doctors in our town wore business suits constantly. Only half a dozen other men experienced such dandy dressing. In times of heavy work load I saw even the president of the Farmers Bank take off his coat and work in his shirtsleeves with suspenders plainly showing. I never saw Doctor Beckett without his coat and double-breasted vest buttoned up snugly, come cold, or come hot. I'm sure he did all his surgery in his best Hart, Schaffner & Marks suit.

Those early day doctors were good, dedicated men, they never shirked their duty. Just imagine on the night of March 13, 1907, about six months before Indian Territory became the State of

Oklahoma, an old doctor road his horse through the rain, out through Dead Man's Slough, over Stoney Point, down into the bottom land and three miles up a muddy rain-hogged road to a small house where he sat up the rest of the night with a young expectant mother who refused to deliver until the next day was breaking.

And for what? It was hardly worth the effort. It was what they called a 'blue baby' and barely tipped the scales at three pounds. It was me.
– *Mack Stanley*

****

Nothin' Ever Happens Around Here

It was a hard way for Uncle Filbert to get the news (everyone says he's as nutty as a Mr. Good Bar). He'd been off on a two week vacation by himself. When he came back he stopped in at my grocery store and asked a neighbor if anything happened while he was gone.

"Naw, nothing ever happens around here." He hesitated a moment and then said, "Hey, wait a minute, there's one piece of news. Your dog died." Fil was upset, "You mean Old Red died! Lordy mercy, how did that happen?"

Fil's friend paused, thought for a moment and said: "I guess it was the burnt horseflesh he ate." "He got it when your barn burned down "The neighbor halted for a moment and then continued. "Actually, the fire started in your house and sparks set the barn and that trapped the horse and then Old Red ate some of the horse flesh that was burnt.

Fil cut in with: "My house burned down too. How did that happen?"

The friend explained," I guess when one of the candles tipped over during the funeral."

"Funeral…at my house?" Fil's voice broke a little, "Who died?"

"Your mother-in-law. You see, when your wife ran off with that traveling salesman, it broke her heart and the poor old lady died. They had the funeral service at the house and that's when the candles caught the curtains afire, then the house and barn went up and killed the horse that Old Red ate some of and died, too. Other than that, nothing happened while you gone." – *Mack Stanley*

****

Questionable Pause

Cousin Larnce went into Stanley's Cafe and was telling everybody about a big fire he's seen that morning.

"It was terrible," he said. "There's never been a fire like that around Spiro." He got his breath and went on. "One of them bird shooters out of Oklahoma City shot at a quail behind the barn, and somehow the wadding out of the shell got m the shingles on Old Doc Crawford's barn and set it on fire. It was like someone poured coal oil on it. The blazes went 30 feet high, and the wind was blowing too. It burned 3,000 bales of Old Doc's prairie hay, and finally the barn burned to the ground. His prize bull was pretty well scorched too. Most terrible thing I ever saw."

You could tell Larnce was taking it hard about all of Old Doc's things burning up and such. He looked like he was worried sick. Everybody else hated it too. Nearly all.

Little Bill from Chitlin Switch, who was enjoying a quiet bowl of good chili, paused in his eating and said: "Did the guy get the quail?"
– *Mack Stanley*

****

Price Checkers Spend More Money Than They Save

Back when we owned our grocery store in Spiro, there was one old gentleman came to our store only when we had a special on Market sausage of four pounds for a dollar. We were supposed to have a limit on our 'ground hog' of four pounds to each customer but this old fellow managed to come through the checkout line three or four times on a busy Saturday. It got so, the wisecracking stock boy called him "Dollar's worth of sausage." Everyone knew who he meant.

I would be the last to say one lady was a bit greedy, but when we ran fresh cabbage as a loss-leader, she always brought her own 100 pound potato sacks to carry her's home. She said: "This is a good time for me to put up my winter kraut. I can't raise cabbage this cheap." She and her kids carried it all off at once and we had to re-order more cabbage.

Uncle Joy from Arkoma always brought a list and spent all day shopping and comparing prices all over town, reading from his purchase order. With his list in hand, his conversation went something like this: "Well Mack, what's your 50 pound sacks of Prize Taker flour going at?" I'd tell him, and he'd make a notation on his list. Moving down, his next question might be, "What's your eight pound buckets of lard going at?" Then another scribble on his list, "Is your Prince Albert still going at two cans for quarter?" Then, "What's your gallon buckets of Rex Jelly going at? What's your Clabber Girl baking Powders gain at?" When he'd exhausted his list and made copious hen tracks with his pencil in his ledger, he would depart without buying anything. As he left he'd call back over his shoulder, "I'll see you later, maybe."

On his way home he always stopped back by, and if he bought only a sack of flour, a bucket of lard and a can of baking powders, we knew without a doubt, that some store in town had beat our "going at" price on Prince Albert, the eight pound buckets of lard and gallons of Rex Jelly, and Griffin's white syrup. – *Mack Stanley*

****

For The Birds

One side of Uncle Oscar's farm bordered on Cache Creek (locally known as Casher Creek), the growth along both sides of this little stream is a tangled mass almost untouched by humans. Aunt Hannah says, "It is just like the Good Lord made it."

There are birds down there in the under bushes like you won't find anywhere else in two states. Red birds, blue birds, yellow birds, orange birds, black and white birds, even some speckled birds. I don't know the names of many of them. They seem to come from everywhere and settle along Old Casher Creek.

A group from the Tulsa Audubon Society came out one day and asked Oscar if it would be all right if they spent the day along the creek in observation. Oscar said he guessed it would be o.k. if they would clean up after themselves and not pollute up the place like the bird hunters from Oklahoma City did.

As these people were leaving for the creek bank, Cousin Larnce came around the corner of the house and asked his father what those people wanted.

Oscar said, "Aw, they're just going to spend all day down on the creek bank and watch the birds."

Larnce, who is not up on the Audubon Society's interest in ornithology, and was now more curious than before, said: "Watch the birds what, Pa?"
– *Mack Stanley*

****

Little Tommy Can Call Your Hand

Since he was two, Tommy, our sister's youngest son, has been able to become sternly-bossy with us elders when we display any lack of knowledge of the way things are with under-age males of his generation. One time I recall vividly was when they came for a visit with us in the desert. I was coming from work and found our nephew and three same-age neighbor boys sitting in the yard, which must have been the biggest sand pile they ever played in. The sand reached as far as the naked eye could see in any direction. They were seated around a small round desert-scarred table under a sun faded and wind tattered big umbrella. They were playing some sort of game with cards. It looked as if they had the remains of several old decks mixed together. I saw at least two racks of spades and three Queens of Hearts.

They had evidently raided Aunt Bess' button box. A small mound of her treasures were piled in front of each of these notorious gamblers. Serious concentration was evident all around the table: The little bidder put one of my wife's jewels in the middle of the table and said "I bet five dollars." The calling of bets went round and round. The bidder called out 'ready' and they ach laid out their hands face up.

One little fellow shouted, "I win! I got the most cards with pictures on em."

"Not so, I got one more'n you got," said another, he is the one who won the pot.

"What kind a game is that, fellows?" I was fool enough to ask. All the little baby-faced boys trying to be big boys looked up at me with such scorn that I felt like an oaf.

"Poker," said the crustiest little guy, spitting in the sand like he'd seen his grandpa do:

My own nephew put the lid on the conversation with: "It's plain ole draw stud poker Uncle Mack. Don't you know nuthin?"""

I made a downcast departure toward the house, hoping the lady there would give me a kinder welcome. – *Mack Stanley*

****

Bad Advice

It crossed my mind that I was pretty fed up with all the henpecking from the lady of the house. When I said so to Little Bill from Chitlin' Switch, he gave me one of his usual "why don't you" answers. He said "Why don't you go home and tell her once and for all who's the boss?" Following Bill's worthy and logical advice, I threw back my shoulders and stomped into the house like a 300 pound fullback and blurted, "What time's supper?" Her calm and steady answer was, "Six-thirty like always."

She must have been shocked when I shouted, "That's not good enough. I want a big steak and baked potato, and I want it by six o'clock. Then lay out my blue serge suit and see if my shoes are shined. I'm going out to the Little Doggie and do me some drinking and dancing."

Bess seemed struck with silence for a spell. Intoxicated with this sudden rush of power, I continued my belligerence: "And when I'm ready for someone to come and tie my new tie for me, you know who's going to do it, don't you?"

"Surely do," said Bess, "That's going to be the man down at the Pleasant Visit Funeral Home!"
– *Mack Stanley*

****

Uncle Doc down at Greenwood says: "There are certain things I cannot do because of circumstances beyond my control" He means his wife won't let him.

****

Everyone in and around Chitlin Switch were pleased that preacher Allstock had influenced Little Bill to be baptized. Hundreds lined both sides of Cache Creek to watch the miracle come to pass.

Finally, the parson doused Bill in the icy water. Amid congratulations Larnce hollered, "Hey, Bill, is that water cold?"

"Not a bit." Bill assured. "Better duck him again preacher," Larnce yelled. "He ain't quit lying yet.
– *Bess Stanley*

****

By The Numbers

Cousin Larnce was not much of a churchgoer. He missed three regular preachers in a row one time.

When he came off the farm and fell in love with all those big yellow bulldozers and Ukes (Euclid dirt movers), and got his first job on the farm-to-market road, he was happy.

Then a big rock fell on one of the workers and killed him. Everyone was deeply saddened by his death. It turned out this fellow had no relatives or close friends so his funeral ceremony fell to the workers.

The boss and all the workers stood around the grave, and no one seemed to know what to do or say. The boss asked for someone to say something from the Bible.

The silence was negative.

The foreman was put out some. He said, "Holy Toledo, don't anyone here know something to say?"

Larnce spoke up: "I passed a town church the other night, and there were lots of people in there. They were pretty noisy. I peeked in, and there was this one guy up front on a platform. He kept saying things over and over."

Exasperated, the boss said, "Well for goodness sake, go ahead and say what he was saying."

Larnce stepped closer to the grave and intoned: "Under B, number six, under O, number forty-four."
– *Mack Stanley*

****

Old Shep Still Had a Big Lick for Uncle Oscar

Uncle Oscar grew too many sweet potatoes one year. He sold some to Spiro merchants and then drove out to Bokoshe to try to unload the rest. He parked in front of a grocery store there and went inside to let them know what nice Puerto Ricans he had for sale.

This grocer had an old car exactly like Ossie's. He also had an old German shepherd dog that was long past the years of having good eyesight, much hearing and almost no sense of smell at all. Well, while Ossie was inside, "Old Shep" made the mistake of somehow clambering up into the back seat of Ossie's old car, no doubt thinking it was his master's. Though I don't really know much about the way an old dog thinks.

It was almost full dark when Oscar finished with the grocer and started home. He was deep in thought about something that happened on the way over here. It was the most unusual thing he had ever experienced: Although he had no radio in his car, for a couple seconds, plainly as he had ever heard, he thought he heard music coming from somewhere in the old jaloppy. Os was thinking defensively now, but he certainly did not intend to tell anyone about this event, too many thought he was already "tetched in the head."

Now, he was driving through the pitch dark, still pretty "spooked" and nervous with the memory of the earlier ghostly music, hoping and praying that same thing would not happen again.

Old Shep, who had been asleep in the dark back seat ever since he came board, woke up, stretched, yawned, and raised himself up putting his big paws on the back of the seat behind Oscar's head and reached his nose over and gave Ossie a good juicy tongue slurping from his shirt collar up over his arm and forward over his eyes.

Our uncle almost went into hysterics, losing control of the old car, going through a garden fence and tearing up Shorty Harris' turnip patch! My shaken old relative was still scared out of his wits and very angry, then he got just plain mean. He made Old Shep walk all the way back to Bokoshe.
– *Mack Stanley*

****

The Meaning of Christmas

My Best Christmas: we were so hard up Mama felt at the end of her rope. She could no longer make a home for herself and us two small kids.

A former neighbor, who had moved out west in Oklahoma was back here for the last wagon load of their household goods. This man and his wife were childless and knowing our predicament he offered to take me back with him and give me a home.

Mama would not consider this at first, but knowing the woman would be like a mother to me, she finally agreed.

I had nothing to say about the arrangement. I felt deserted. I felt like I was being given away. But there was no apparent alternative. I was not all for it, but went along. What could I do? I was only seven years old.

This man had wooden rim and bows covered with canvas over his load of household plunder. We began the 140 mile journey behind two big brown mules. It was at the beginning of December and seemed to rain the whole trip.

The way the mules walked and flopped their long ears in unison and pulled the wagon through a sea of mud grew boring to watch and seemed to take forever to get anywhere. The trip took ten days.

Finally, we came to the town. It was even smaller than Spiro. The name of this new town was Cairo, like that big town in Egypt. You know how they pronounce that city. But we pronounced this one like Karo Syrup, Oklahoma style.

These folks lived two miles on through town and I had to walk to school in town. Of course, I had my first day fist fight with the school bully and lost that battle too.

I could soon see these folks had not improved their lot much by the 140 mile move. Still, I had a good warm bed and plenty of food. The main thing I recall about this lady's cooking was her molasses cake. It was big and super delicious. All her other food was only excellent. She would pass for a second mother, but she was not Mama.

All I remember about the school was it was on a low hill, hardly more than a knoll at the edge of the small town, and the first day bully challenger had a good left jab. On my way back and forth each day, I encountered some of the biggest jackrabbits I ever saw. With my young and unjaded imagination I easily turned them into wild Kangaroos. This was a jungle and lions and tigers lurked just out of sight along the road in this distant land.

On my second Sunday morning there, two days before Christmas, a strange Model T Ford pulled up in the yard and Mama got out and hurried toward the porch. Before she reached the house, arms out stretched, she cried out to the three of us: "I just can't go through with it."

She held her arms out to me and said "We may starve in the future, but we'll starve together.'

I felt proud and renewed and whole again. I ran to meet her and responded with, "Yes Mama. Together." – *Mack Stanley*

****

Mack's Favorite Christmas Story

It was a cold day with leaden overcast sky. The whistling wind made it seem colder. It was Christmas Eve back in the Big Depression. Very few expensive gifts would be exchanged around here tomorrow, but everyone was looking forward to the great day.

From the cozy inside of the drugstore where I worked, I watched the tale unfold. I saw Jake Brewer pull in beside Redwine's big hardware store and unhitch his team of mules. Jake had brought a load of firewood to town to sell. I knew that although Jake's small family had enough food to winter on, and reasonably warm clothes, most likely there was not now a dime cash on the place. My guess was he wanted to sell the rick of wood to buy some little store-bought present for his wife and little kids.

I saw Jake stamp his feet and walk about swinging his arms and hug himself to keep from freezing. His breath came out in the cold air in white plumes, but Jake never deserted his post to even go to the lunch room, or even eat a snack at the wagon.

By 4:30 that afternoon Jake had no luck. The sky had become darker and the wind colder than ever. With the threat of early dark and snow beginning to fall, I saw Jake begin to hitch his mules back to the still-loaded wagon.

I walked out there across the wide street to where Jake was making the final hooks of the harness. I didn't really need a load of wood, but it was something that wouldn't spoil and could always be used later on. Jake was about to climb up on the wagon. As I walked up to Jake I said, "You haven't had much luck selling your wood, I see."

Jake said, "No, I been here all day, and braced everyone who came along. They have either spent all their money for Christmas, or just don't want any wood. I'll just have to haul it back home, I guess."

I had watched Jake half freeze our there all day from my warm place and I guess the Christmas feeling had gotten to me a little. I told Jake I'd be willing to pay him the going price for it, but he might not want to deliver it to our house about a mile up on the hill.

Jake put on a big grin and said, "Mister, you got yourself a deal. Right now, I'd deliver this load of wood anywhere in the whole township for the going price of one dollar!"

Merry Christmas...

– *Mack Stanley*

****

Forty Winks on Christmas Eve

A Christmas memory: We had moved to town, but Uncle Oscar and Aunt Hannah still lived out in the country. One Christmas they came to visit us, and we were so broke we didn't even have any store coupons. We kids had already heard a rumor that Santa's reindeer ran away with his sled on a practice run and he might not be well enough to come to our house.

With no money, we all could spend was the time together, but Aunt Hannah had brought a lot of home canned goodies, so we would at least have a great feast. Somehow, Mama had hoarded a four bit piece, She unwrapped it with her small handkerchief and sent me to Scott's Meat Market for two pounds of sausage for Christmas breakfast. This was Mr. Scott's best grade of groundhog and it went at four pounds for a dollars.

When we kids all bedded down on pallets in the front room, we all had that store bought sausage on our minds. That made it a hard matter to go to sleep. Forty winks were the most any of us got that night.

A neighbor came home from the Dixie Theatre about 10 o'[clock and woke us wide awake drawing water from his well with a squeaky rope pulley. We thought it was morning and sausage time. Once up, we exchanged what few gifts we had while the giant breakfast of sausage, eggs, country fries and cat head size biscuits was being cooked. After the big meal, we sat around waiting for daylight to come. We waited and waited, but no daylight. Aunt Hannah, who was trembly and emotional under the least stress, decided the world was coming to an end. She had us all down on our knees ready to pray when a knock came at the front door. It was the neighbor whose rusty pulley had squeaked us awake three hours before. He said, "I saw the lights on and reckoned someone was sick. Is there anything I can do?" He looked around and said, "What are you all doing down on the floor?"

When Uncle Oscar asked him what time it was, he said, "1 A.M."

With this reprieve, Aunt Hannah became her old self again and became belligerent with the Good Samaritan: "Why don't you grease that rusty old well pulley of yours and quit waking folks up in the middle of the night?"

Other than that it was a great Christmas!
– *Mack Stanley*

****

Mack's Christmas Memories

The first Christmas I can recall in much detail has to be one of my best memories. I must have been about seven and fully able to tag along with Mama down to the business district of Spiro. This proud little urban area consisted of two very large general mercantile stores surrounded by maybe 40 smaller business establishments of any and every kind that could make a living there. Our town sat squatted on the prairie like two old setting hens surrounded by about 40 baby chicks clustered around them.

Mama could always spend a lot of time looking in the stores but never had much money to spend. She could put in overtime looking in the large places which had anything you might desire, but her favorite place was a smaller variety store we chose to call "The Racket Store." Don't ask me why.

On this day I remember so well just before Christmas Day, she gave me a dime for the Dixie Theater, probably her way of getting rid of me for a while. I saw a double Western with William S. Hart and Dustin Farnum as stars, an episode of a Pearl White cliffhanger and a newsreel. When I got back to the Racket Store Mama was still looking. That time through, she had a good-sized package and several smaller ones. For some reason or other that big odd shaped package aroused my curiosity. I had been telling her since last New Year's Day just what I wanted for Christmas. After my wheedling and pestering her all the way back to our small house, she finally admitted: "Yes, the large package is your Christmas gift, but young man if you keep plaguing me about it I swear I'll give it to some other little boy. Don't you mention it again." I could tell by the near tremor in her scolding voice that I'd better settle down.

That was the longest rest-of-the-day I ever put in, and the next day was longer than my whole life before had been. In that paralyzed due course of time it was Christmas Day. I was first in the family to get my gift unwrapped and it was a joy. It was what I had been wishing for more than a whole year. Miracles never ceased! Lordy, it was my very own play set of garden tools. A hoe, a shovel and a rake, little ones, but almost like Papa's. Breakfast was forgotten. I rushed out to the garden plot to try out my own tools! Papa had to make dire threats, including brandishing a small limb from a peach tree, to get me in there for ham & eggs with biscuits and country-fried potatoes.

That toy garden set began the cultivation of my love for working outside. I still have that.

Garden tools are expensive now, but the set I loved so much and got me started, cost .35 ¢.

Merry Christmas, from Mack & Bess

****

Christmas At 18

At eighteen, I felt the world was created expressly for me and others I was growing up with. I was "going with" a pretty girl in our home town. Her father, the preacher, did not approve of me. He thought his daughter was way too good for me, but as months of our relationship passed, our closeness caused us to be referred to as "pledged." Then, I went off to my first grown-up job at a market in the boomtown of Kilgore, Texas. Our parting was tearful, but I promised to come back for her at Christmas, and she promised to wait for me. We felt we were engaged.

In my new surroundings, I met another girl as pretty as the one back home. Besides she was there. In the way of all flesh, I fell for his new Miss's with all the fervor of a new beginning. With a new job, new friends and a new girl, I was really on my way.

But something was wrong. I was bothered. My promise to the girl back home was bothering my conscience. Finally, there was nothing but to go back and tell her I had found a love stronger than ours had been. I went back home on Christmas Eve.

I was nervous as an outlaw in church as I got off the Fort Smith and Western, and still had a mile to walk and agonize over just how to explain my fickle heart to the deserted sweetheart. How could I let her down with the least heartbreak? I must not hurt her more than I had. I was nothing but a cad.

This lovely girl met me at the door with an embrace. Was there a stirring of my old feelings? Then I got hold of myself, trying to make this no more hurtful for her. I saw myself as loathsome. I tried to get started on my confession, but only a few mumbles came out. She held up her hand to halt my mumbling effort to tell my fickle tale. "Before you speak," she said, "I must tell you something shocking. I'm getting married tomorrow. My finance came to town right after you left. He works for the telephone company, and we are moving to Tahlequah on our wedding day."

I feigned my own case of heartbreak, let her see a crocodile tear or two and got out of there. By the time I was outside, one or two tears seemed real. Now, I felt like I was the one betrayed.

"Oh well," I sighed to myself, "that's life ... But there is still Texas." – *Mack Stanley*

****

Little Bill from Chitlin' Switch thinks everyone celebrates as ruggedly as he does at New Year. He always sends "Get Well" cards at that time. He's the one who plays Frisbee with manhole covers. Happy New Year!

– *Mack Stanley*

****

Sissy's Christmas Trickery

When we lived down on North Fourth Street in Fort Smith and Sissy and I went to Belle Grove School, our Christmas celebrations were less than bountiful. We were so poor, that if we had had mice, they would have had to go to a nearby church and try to beg non existent food from their mice. Being poor didn't seem to bother me too much. Why should it? Poor was all I had ever known, but somehow it hurt Sissy. She seemed to comprehend more than I that there was a better lot out there than ours. I suppose I knew some other folks had more than we did, but that was just the way things were. I could live with that but it seemed different with my sister. As Sissy grew, she became dishonest enough to exaggerate how well-off we were. When she reached dating age, there was a certain boy from Tulsa she did not want to know how poor we were. This boy was visiting in Fort Smith through Christmas holidays and dating Sissy.

There was a fashionable apartment building up on Sixth Street, and she would walk the two blocks up there in the back door and down the hall to the front door. Then, when her date drove up front, Sissy would trip gaily out to the car and greet her date like she was just dashing down from her nice apartment.

This boyfriend soon suspected something, because he'd never been invited in. He didn't quite buy the tale that she had to slip out to date him. He figured to find out just what was wrong. He watched her come out the back door and followed her on foot to see where she went. Then he guessed why she did this. The much less than modest, small and drab house told him her story. The next time they had a date this boy parked and met her at the back door of the apartments. Sissy almost died of embarrassment. She was stunned speechless. She had fibbed and she was caught! She survived only because the boy chose to say nothing about the trick she had been playing. They went on their date as if nothing out of the ordinary had happened, and he took her to her own door when the date was over. For his next date he came to our little old house, went in and met our parents and everyone liked everyone.

No, they did not get married and live happily ever after. After the Christmas holidays the boy went back to Tulsa, and Sissy went to other boys.

But she never played that fancy apartment trick on anyone else. – *Mack Stanley*

****

Based On O'Henry's "Gift Of The Magic"

George and Mary were a young married couple. They were deeply in love with one another. George had a job at Harrison's General Mercantile, but times were bad and $40 a month was all a job like his paid. More than half of his salary went for food and rent. The remainder seldom lasted out the month. Dollars were scarce as duck's teeth. But Christmas was in a few days and both of these young people would be devastated if they could not give one another something at Christ's birth time.

Mary knew that George's most prized possession was his grandfather's old pocket watch, and she wanted to buy him a nice new fob for it.

On other hand, George knew that Mary's long beautiful hair was her pride joy. His plan was to buy her a beautiful jeweled comb to set it off.

No money was forthcoming from outside, so each knew they would have to depend on their own resources, so drastic steps were taken: Mary cut and sold her beautiful tresses to buy a fob for George's watch. And George hocked his grandfather's watch to be able to buy a beautiful comb for Mary's hair. Each of these deeds now completely nullified the gift from the other. What a bad surprise. Nevertheless they fell into each others arms with hugs and kisses.

The young people's gift did not come from 'the wise men from the east.' Their gift was totally unselfish love for one another, and that gift came straight from God. – *Mack Stanley*

****

People Helping People in Many Ways

It was late in the year of 1931. The Big Depression (anyone who was there will confirm that there was nothing 'Great' about it) had brought everything to a halt in our broad land. The Seminole oil boom field had been deserted. Oil was on the skids. The shop foreman near where I lived had been booted out of his job, but had fallen heir to the fine job of changing all the colors of Prairie Gas and Oil stations in Corpus Christi, Texas to Pure Oil Company's colors. I could go with him as a painter at .40¢ an hour. So I went, and I painted service stations. There were so many of us on this job we finished it in several weeks. Hard times again, and Christmas was just around the corner.

That was when I heard from Little Sister, in the nearby Rio Grande Valley. They had finally starved out as custodians of a fledgling orange grove there. Her father, Charley had the Opportunity to build a sewer disposal plant in Westville, Oklahoma. If Sister's husband and yours truly would be there on the day after Christ's Birthday we could start as form builder's. Pay was .25¢ an hour. Eight hours, two bucks.

I rode in the cold turtle seat of Sister's 1927 Ford Roadster and the front riders had no curtains to protect them. We began the journey with one quart of Musselman's Apple Butter and three loaves of bread. By the time we reached Fort Smith, Arkansas, we had not eaten in more than 24 hours, the gas tank was flat empty and we didn't have enough pennies total to buy a Nickel sack of Bull Durham. And it was Christmas.

We had lived in Fort Smith in a previous lifetime, and I recalled my friend there, Joe Wade. Joe came to us at once and turned his pockets inside out in earnestness. They produced two well-worn dollar bills. Joe offered us half his fortune. He said that much gas in our tank would get us on into Westville with flying colors.

With tears in my eyes I lamented: "But Joe, we're starving"

Joe already had his thinking cap on that day and almost shouted, "No problem. I can take care of that too. Drive this flivver up to North Seventh Street!"

We went up on Seventh Street to an old building that looked like an old church. It was the Salvation Army. Joe led us in like he owned the place. And never were we treated more like royalty, nor given a better feast, with a paper poke full to take along. Joe's dollar's worth of gasoline enabled us to get to Westville and those jobs.

I have never stopped loving the Salvation Army since that day. I have sent a few dollars whenever I could.

Did I ever repay Joe Wade his dollar bill? Yes sir, I most certainly did.

Merry Christmas & Happy New Year!

— Mack Stanley

****

About The Authors

Mack Stanley, born March 13, 1907 in Indian Territory, Oklahoma wrote thousands of humorous stories, articles, anecdotes, jokes and puns for newspapers and print media for most of life in the small eastern Oklahoma town of Spiro.

Mack could have been a ghost writer for the famous Cherokee cowboy Will Rogers during the 1930s. Mack lived in California during the 1930s, the heyday years of Will Rogers.

Mack may have been the re-incarnation of Will Rogers. When he moved back to Oklahoma in the 1940s, he built a house on Alaska Street in Spiro, where he wrote most of his published articles.

Bess (Gist) Stanley was born at Fort Coffee. Oklahoma on January 21, 1919, she and Mack were married in Las Vegas, Nevada, July 13, 1939. The couple lived in Spiro most of their lives, except a few short years in California during the depression, late 1930s and into the 1940s.

For several years, Mack wrote a weekly column, known as "Hometown Tales" in the Spiro Graphic up until 1995, when health issues began to take a toll on his writing.

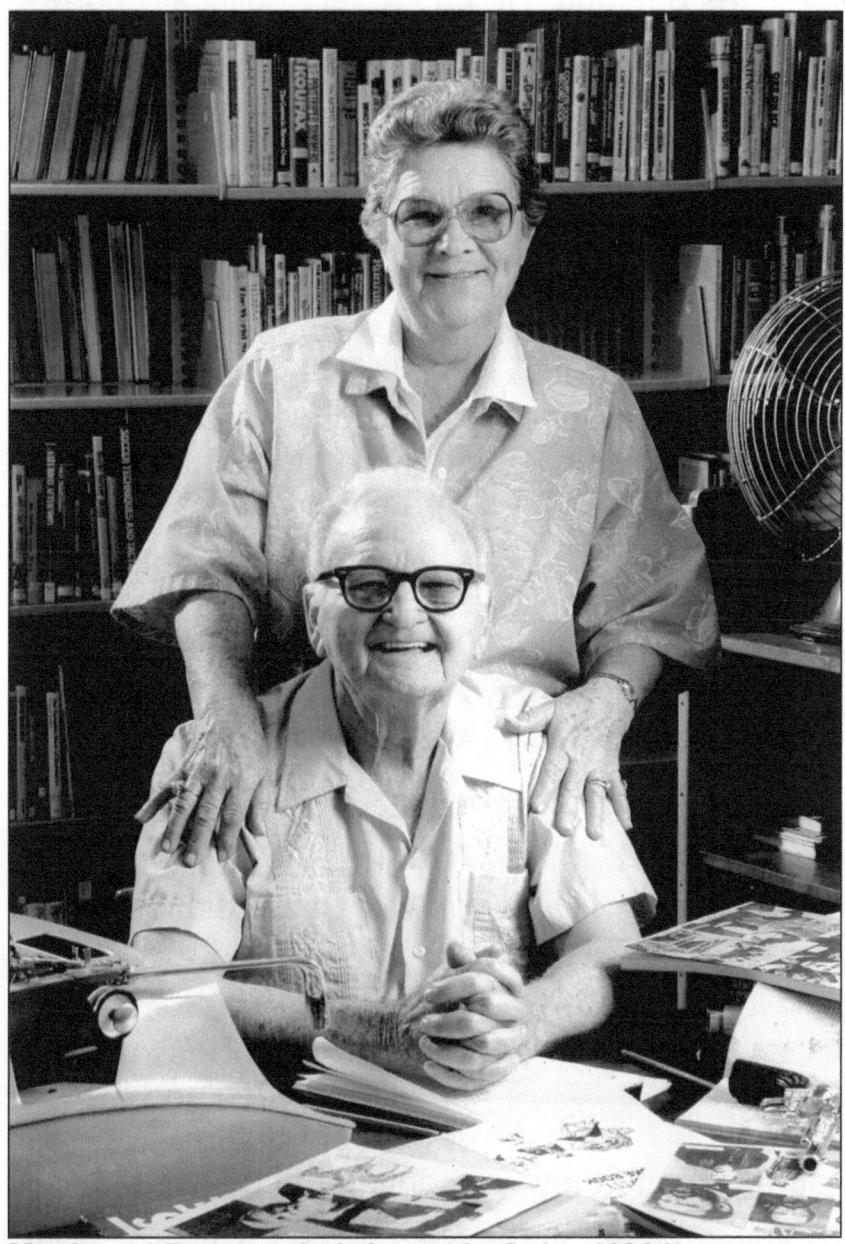

Mack and Bess at their home in Spiro (1991)

Mack's stories and articles, with input from his lovely wife, Bess, always made one chuckle, sometimes out loud. He had a very politically correct way of describing the physical short comings and nature of people.

His stories make one feel like you are right there or a part of the event as if you were a part of what happened or watched it happen.

Mack is a published author of several books and magazine articles about the early years of Spiro and during the great depression. His 'Hometown Tales', published in the Spiro Graphic, bring back many of these stories, compiled into two volumes for one's reading pleasure.

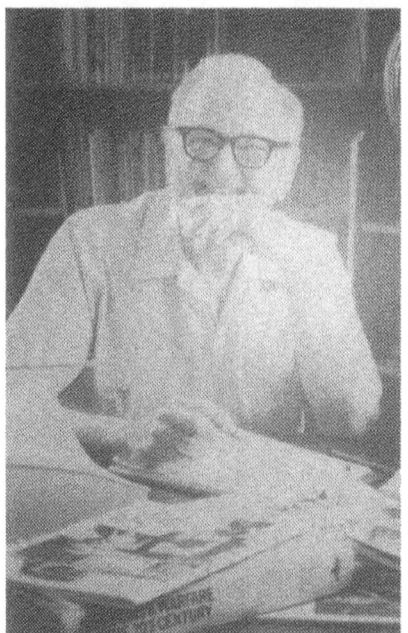

Mack Stanley died on March 30, 1996 at the age of 89, suffering from complications of cancer. The Spiro Graphic published a front page article and tribute to Mack's accomplishments in life. Bess Stanley died September 4, 2001 at the age of 82.

Mack and Bess were well respected and loved members of the community, and they will continue to be missed.

Both lay in rest at the New Hope Cemetery, east of Spiro on U.S. 271 Highway.

About The Authors

John Clark has been writing and publishing newspapers for 25 years, mostly in the small town of Spiro, Oklahoma, located in the Arkansas River Valley near the border town of Fort Smith, Arkansas.

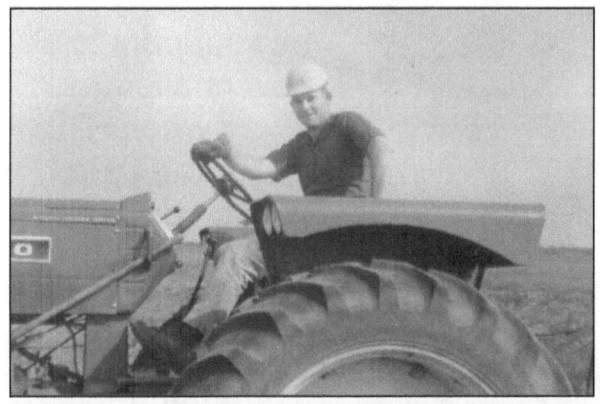 Clark graduated from Northeastern State University in Tahlequah, Oklahoma in 1972, earning a bachelors degree in History and Political Science. The Journalism degree comes from the 'school of hard knocks' with over 30 years of radio broadcasting, newspaper writing and finally a chance to tell short humorous stories about real people without having to make up or create a phony reality TV show.

John grew up in the southwest, born in San Antonio, Texas in 1946, and lived in Oklahoma and Arkansas most of his life.

As a young boy growing up in northeastern Oklahoma, he remembers real-life experiences of raising and showing livestock at the county fairs and the older kids taking him 'snipe' hunting after dark. Kids growing up in the 1950s watched very little television if any.

As one of many early baby boomers, he graduated from high school in the mid-60's and took his senior trip to California, and overseas during the Vietnam War, serving three years in the United States Marine Corps.

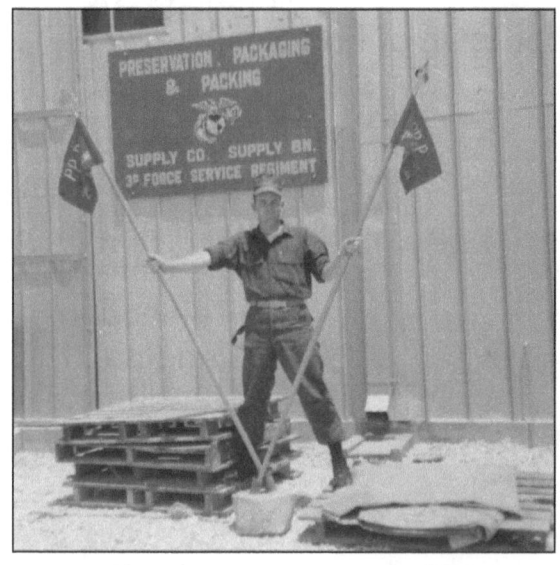

Writing and producing small town weekly newspapers is a new challenge every week. The basic rules are: publish or perish in the newspaper business.

John has written and produced feature stories about major league baseball players down to the little league. He's interviewed thousands of athletes, written thousands game stories for small schools.

He has written about high-profile murder cases in Oklahoma for over 20 years, chased down traffic fatalities; followed high-speed police chases, witnessed drug busts and continues to write about corrupt elected officials from the state capitol to city hall.

Clark is the Editor and General Manager of the Spiro Graphic, a weekly hometown newspaper that answers the phones with real live people and publishes free obituaries for families with relatives having ties to the local area.

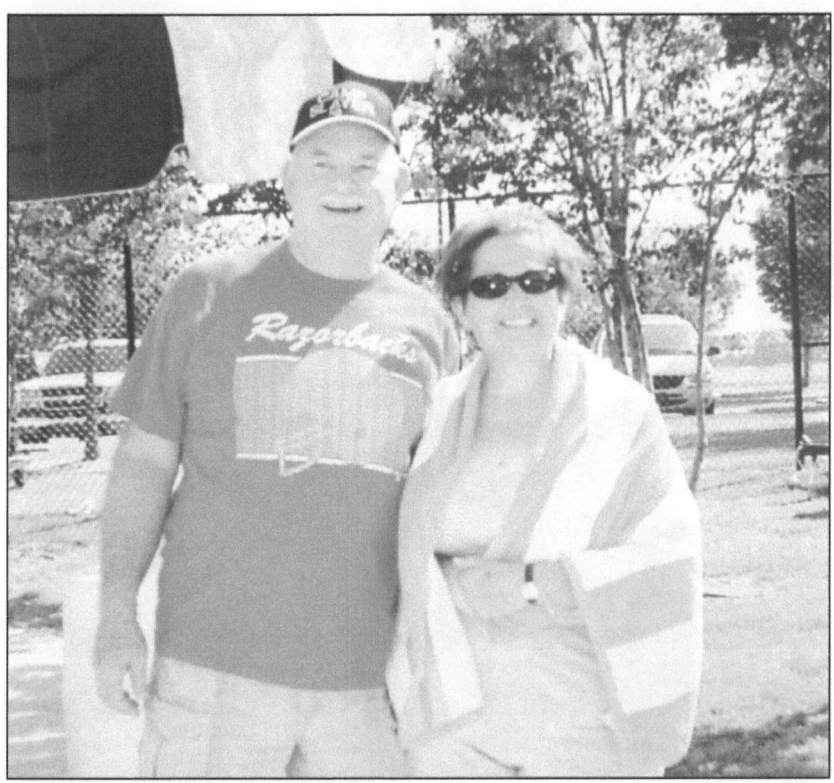

John and his wife Debby.